A Christian View of Homosexuality

A Christian View of Homosexuality

John W. Drakeford

BROADMAN PRESS
Nashville, Tennessee

4256-20
ISBN: 0-8054-5620-1

Dewey Decimal Classification: 261.834
Subject heading: HOMOSEXUALITY

Library of Congress Catalog Card Number: 76-41474
Printed in the United States of America

Contents

About the Author

Dr. John W. Drakeford is a graduate of six institutions
of higher learning, has published twenty-three books, and
is a psychologist licensed by the Texas State Board of
Examiners of Psychologists. He also serves as a supervisor
of the Association of Clinical Pastoral Educators and as a
clinical member and supervisor of the American Association
of Marriage and Family Counselors. The father of two sons,
he and his wife are constantly traveling in order to conduct
Family Enrichment Conferences. He presently serves at
Southwestern Baptist Theological Seminary as professor
of psychology and director of the marriage and family
counseling center.

A Christian View of Homosexuality

1. One Man's Story

A deeply religious person, he held the position of minister of music in a church; and on Sundays, Wednesdays, and the nights of regular church meetings, he was the epitome of a theologically conservative Christian minister. Other nights of the week he became the aggressive homosexual searching for partners, making regular rendezvous, visiting gay bars, and finally "coming out" (making his gayness known) . . . . This double life proved to be a precarious existence.

What a sight I made! Thoroughly humiliated. All my pride and self-sufficiency gone. Pleading for mercy.

My white shirt and blue slacks, so immaculate a brief hour before, were now covered with dirt and muck from sprawling facedown in that filthy alley. My hands and arms were dirty, scraped and etched with wavy patterns of gravel rash; and tiny globules of blood oozed through the coating of dirt.

Lost without glasses, I wanted desperately to reach down and pick them up, but I couldn't bear the thought of bending my aching body. The blood seeped through the front of my shirt and spread a strange series of red inkblot patterns.

What a difference a few hours can make. Earlier that day I had driven along the highways as if I owned the world. The sun shone down from an azure sky, flecked with cotton candy clouds. A shower had washed the countryside, making more vivid the contrast of yellow and gold balls of fruit against the shining green backdrop of the citrus groves. My

tires *drummed out a pleasant rhythm as I raced along the*
freeway with a sense of freedom from the responsibilities
of work and home.

The church music conference wasn't due to start until
the following morning, but I wanted to get there early and
have a look around the town. Wandering around a town
away from where I lived had become increasingly enjoy-
able to me.

After checking in at the motel, I ate a leisurely meal.
Later I decided to take a walk, but I didn't meet anyone
I knew; so I decided to go to the movies.

Once inside the theater I took a seat at the end of a row.
Just a few seats away from me was a nice-looking young
man about nineteen years old. I lost interest in the movie
and decided to make an approach to him.

I began to fondle myself, and out of the corner of my
eye I could see that he was watching me. In a few moments
he got up and walked along the row in my direction. Slid-
ing across me into the aisle, he walked to the back of the
theater.

My attention returned to the picture until I realized that
he had returned down the aisle and was kneeling beside me.
In a quiet voice he said, "Come to the back with me. I
want to talk with you."

With that he stood up and walked back up the aisle.
Petrified, I didn't move . . . maybe he would give up
and leave the theater

A few minutes passed and then I sensed that he was back. This time there was a threatening note in his voice. "Come back here. I want to talk with you." He retreated once again.

There was just one thing for me to do—run for it.

Jumping to my feet, I ran to the exit door and raced like mad down the street, spurred on by the sound of the enraged youth in hot pursuit.

As I ran down the sidewalk, I noticed a dark alley behind the big building on the other side of the street. I changed direction, shot across the street, and headed for that dark spot, convinced that it would offer a place to hide.

As I rushed into the welcoming darkness, something hit me. Wham! I felt as if a giant fist had belted me in the chest and knocked me to the ground. Someone had strung a chain across that entrance, and I had charged right in it.

I lay winded on the pavement; and my pursuer, his breath coming in gasps, stood triumphantly over me. Searing pain told me that my body was skinned from my chest to the base of my stomach.

He reached down and grabbed my arm. "Come on and get up. I'm taking you to the police."

Slowly and painfully I climbed to my feet, but the aching of my body was overruled by the awful fear of being arrested and put in jail.

"Everybody saw what you were doing."

"No, they didn't—nobody saw me but you."

"Well, I'm taking you to the police."

I begged and pleaded with him not to do that; and when he seemed to hesitate, I began to gain confidence that he wouldn't carry through with his threat.

He looked thoughtful and said, "I've had a little bit of experience in talking with people like you," and he began to ask me questions—how I got started; how long I had been active; whether I was married. When I admitted that I was married and had a child, he made a startling suggestion. "Why don't you tell your wife about this?"

"Oh, I couldn't."

"Do you feel that she loves you?"

"Yes."

"If she loves you, she will understand and will help you overcome it. Tell her—just share your secret with her."

His suggestion dramatized the strange relationship between Marian and me. Both of us were terribly ignorant about certain aspects of sexuality, and in my case my lack of knowledge may have stemmed in part from my family background and early relationships with females. These factors, however, were not the sole causes of my behavior.

About two years later Marian and I went to a convention in a nearby city. The conference divided into smaller subgroups, and Marian and I were in different groups. One afternoon she went to her group, but mine did not meet; so I had time on my hands. I decided to go to a movie.

Entering the darkness, I stood at the back and waited until my eyes accommodated themselves. I looked down and saw a young man sitting alongside the wall where there were just two seats. I sat down beside him so that he was sort of hemmed in against the wall. I "accidentally" let my hand fall on his leg. He moved it. Not far because he couldn't.

After a while I repeated the gesture. He reached over, grabbed me by the neck of the shirt, jumped to his feet, and forcibly pulled me out of the seat. He half dragged me up the aisle and told the usher that I was making advances to him. The usher called the police, and an officer arrived shortly afterward. They took me to the station.

Of course I denied anything and everything. The officer who talked with me was rather sympathetic, and I felt he knew what he was doing. He lectured me, suggesting that I seek psychiatric help, and tried to get me to talk. But I admitted nothing.

They finally charged me with disturbing the peace and allowed me to call my wife. When Marian arrived at the jail, I told her that nothing had happened, but I don't think that she believed me. The policeman who had been very helpful also talked with Marian. I'm sure he expressed his feelings to her.

*Because they were unable to get in touch with anyone
who could determine the fine, I spent the night in jail. It
was really rotten for Marian. She had to go back to the
hotel and spend the night by herself. When she came back
to the police station the next morning, they contacted the
judge, who said the fine would be one hundred dollars—
cash.*

*Again the brunt of it all fell on Marian. She had to call
some friends on the pretext that we had car trouble and
needed money to pay the repair bill. She looked rather
grim as she paid out the money and they turned me loose.*

*Later, in a painful confrontation, Marian told me that
if anything ever happened again she would leave me. This
was nearly two years after I had originally told her about
my homosexuality. I felt that inside she was fearful that
I was playing my homosexual games, but she wanted to
believe me that nothing had happened.*

*All the same, it became a barrier between us. I never
shared anything else with her. She had said she would
leave me, and the threat hung over my head.*

In these words Jeff J. tells about the dilemma of his life
as he moved in and out of the "gay" world. A well-built,
handsome man with an outgoing personality, in his early
thirties at this time, and the father of three children, Jeff
is fluent and persuasive of speech. A college graduate in
music, he has done some work on a graduate study program. By profession he was a minister of music in a church,

a position which he held for some ten years. Fairly successful in his work, he wasn't altogether happy about the trivia
of church life.

During this period of time our paths had crossed. I had
spoken in a church where he had served as a minister, and I
met both Jeff and his wife. The meeting was casual and
made no lasting impression on me. The next time I met
Jeff he was attending therapy groups at the counseling center of which I am the director. When he had arrived he'd
been interviewed by one of our counselors and one night
sought an interview with me. He reminded me of our meeting years before and related the story of the strange odyssey
that had led him to this moment.

That ten-year period had produced a series of experiences
rivalling the memorable exploits of Robert Louis Stevenson's
Dr. Jekyll and Mr. Hyde.

A deeply religious person, he held the position of minister of music in a church; and on Sundays, Wednesdays, and
the nights of regular church meetings, he was the epitome
of a theologically conservative Christian minister. Other
nights of the week he became the aggressive homosexual
searching for partners, making regular rendezvous, visiting
gay bars, and finally "coming out" (making his gayness
known). These two roles were separately maintained, and
he proudly claimed he'd never had any sexual contacts with
a person belonging to a church where he served.

This double life proved to be a precarious existence. In
his role as minister he warned his young people about the
hazards of smoking and drinking, yet followed these practices as he moved around the bars of the gay world. On
occasions he was pursued, arrested, attacked, blackmailed.
It all moved to a dramatic confrontation when he was

arrested and charged with committing a homosexual act with a juvenile. For this offense he was imprisoned on a penal farm.

While in prison Jeff had written out his story in longhand in three exercise books. He loaned these books to me; and as I read them, I felt they constituted a remarkable record of a man's inner perceptions of a series of unfortunate events that had befallen him. I later spent hours interviewing Jeff. These conversations were recorded.

The result is what I consider a remarkable personal document. In this present writing I intend to use Jeff J.'s actual words as much as possible. Hopefully we have two major types of materials: that which comes from books, articles, and experiences in therapy groups, and other resources reporting about homosexuality. In addition, we have one man's perception of himself as a homosexual. Throughout the writings the statements of Jeff J. will be in italics to distinguish his personal statements from my exposition on the subject.

Further, this book treats the lives of both male and female homosexuals (lesbians).

2. The "Coming Out" of the Gay Movement

"Coming out," the step a homosexual takes in making an open declaration of his homosexuality, has always been looked upon as a special experience; and now it seemed as if the whole movement "came out" with a new aggressive attitude. The term "gay" came to the fore, and the militant gay movement mushroomed.

The cover page of *Time* magazine has featured many important newsmakers. The January issue each year has pictured *Time's* "Man of the Year," and many a solid citizen has enjoyed armchair contesting with *Time* as to who has influenced the whole world for better or for worse in the past twelve months.

Though not a "man of the year," a new "celebrity" appeared in 1975. The September 8 edition featured the picture of Sergeant Leonard Matlovich with a terse statement: "I am a homosexual." The cover story was a long article that used the incident of the Air Force sergeant's court-martial as a beginning point for an article about the gay world and the rights of the homosexuals.

A homosexual's gaining notice on the cover of *Time* was rather significant. We might note, in passing, that just two weeks later the honored spot was occupied by Lynette Alice (Squeaky) Fromme, the follower of Charles Manson who had attempted to assassinate President Ford. Nevertheless, the place of prominence with the "coming out" statement of Sergeant Matlovich, in which he declared himself to be gay, is characteristic of a new aggressive attitude for homosexuals, who, in past generations, have been most careful to keep their sexual preference hidden.

This new attitude of homosexuals is a direct extension of the protest movements of the sixties, when various groups began demonstrating for their rights, to be followed in rapid succession by the protestors against the Vietnam War. When in 1969 the police in New York City closed down a homosexual bar in Greenwich Village, the bar's patrons fought back and battled with the police, setting fires, fistfighting, and hurling bricks. This incident was the beginning of the rapid radicalization of the homosexual movement.

"Coming out," the step a homosexual takes in making an open declaration of his homosexuality, has always been looked upon as a special experience; and now it seemed as if the whole movement "came out" with a new aggressive attitude. The term "gay" came to the fore, and the militant gay movement mushroomed. Organizations like the Gay Liberation Front grew until today there are some eight hundred gay organizations. These groups are even attracting the attention of the academic community; some fifty colleges include gay studies in their curriculums.

After coming out, the gay organizations took a leaf out of the books of civil rights movements and set about to change local or state laws which they perceived as discriminating against homosexuals. The defiant note was dramatized by a mother who carried a placard reading, "My son is gay, and that's okay." Many homosexuals demonstrated, singing the civil rights song "We Shall Overcome." Although these methods have been imitations of civil rights groups, only a vivid imagination could equate the gay enterprise with the long fight of blacks against discrimination.

Among the homosexual objects of attack stood the church, which had traditionally taken a strong stand against homosexuality. But as the movement gained momentum, its attitude toward the church took a subtle change. Apparently many of the gays felt the need for the solace of religion, for they seemed to have adopted the motto "If you can't beat 'em, join 'em."

Liberals in the religious establishment, who are never happy with any strong traditional stands, welcomed the gays. They assumed that the gay movement was, after all, an issue of social justice and that the church needed to be on the proper side. Gaining fresh courage, homosexuals within the various mainline churches began to form gay caucuses and set up gay organizational gatherings. The nation's leading gay newspaper suddenly had some new advertisers, as religious gays appealed to their fellow gays in forming pressure groups to push for recognition within their respective religious denominations.

Despite all of this, the conservative denominations still strongly resisted and declared themselves against any acceptance of homosexuality; but they are now confronted with a new challenge. One Pentecostal pastor with fundamentalist doctrine had left his wife and church to declare his homo sexual orientation. He launched himself on what must have seemed an impossible combination as he wedded a *fundamentalist theology* with *homosexual ethics.* The church he founded was originally called the Sodomy Church; but as it grew in strength, it sought a new respectability and changed its name to the more acceptable Metropolitan Community Church. The church entered on a period of rapid growth as it spread across the country.

This new leader marched into battle, Bible in hand, to

lead the homosexual forces onward. As in any religious group, there are members who take different attitudes toward the Scriptures; but typically the really aggressive groups are those with more conservative attitudes toward the Bible. This attitude is seen in an incident in which a columnist in a gay paper, *The Catalyst,* called the inspiration of the Scriptures into question. The editor quickly responded, "Every portion of the Old and New Testament—every single verse in every chapter of every book—is most definitely the divinely inspired Word of God." [1]

Whereas people who have a liberal view of the Bible have had no difficulty in rejecting those portions of the Bible that don't suit their point of view, it is another matter for a group to use the Scriptures to prove to their satisfaction that the church has, for nearly two thousand years, been completely mistaken in its view of sexual ethics.

So has arisen a movement which calls into question the *exegesis* of a large number of Bible passages. To carry out an exegesis means to "draw out" the true meaning of a Bible passage. In my days as a theological student, we used to speak about "eisegesis"—a technique whereby, instead of drawing out, the expositor "read in" his own particular point of view. The question we now face is whether the homosexuals are really indulging in exegesis or eisegesis.

The whole situation has taken a new turn. In times past, the issue of homosexuality was summarily dismissed as a perversion which the Bible condemned. This, however, is a day in which many of these judgments have been called into question and we must clarify a number of issues. Some of these include:

What is a homosexual?
How do people get this way?
What about the female homosexual, the lesbian?
What does the Bible teach?
Is gay good?
Can a homosexual change?
Is there a propaganda push?
What should the church do?

3. Who Is Homosexual?

There have probably been more false stereotypes concerning sexuality than concerning any other types of human activity. Extreme forms range from the sissy, limp-wristed male, with his effeminate speech, to the solidly built woman in her mannish clothes, devoid of all soft feminine traits. These physical characteristics may be no indication at all of sexual orientation. A homosexual male may be strong and rugged in appearance, and the female (lesbian) soft, tender, and the essence of apparent femininity.

Who are these people who have been known in the past as "homosexuals," "queers," or by a variety of other names, but who prefer, for rather obvious reasons, the euphemistic term gay? The dictionary defines their condition as:

homosexuality—ho·mo·sex·u·al·i·ty (ho me-sek she-wal e-te, ho-me) n. Sexual desire or behavior directed toward a person or persons of one's own sex.

Of course, this is a grave oversimplification. This attraction can be of varying degrees, involving everything from casual sexual contacts to a deep involvement with another person and a commitment to a whole life-style that may have some awesome social and political implications.

Trying to come to terms with these considerations, Kinsey, the sex researcher, came up with a six-point scale on which a person's status could be judged. The scale numbered from zero to six, and the designations ranged from exclusively homosexual (6) to exclusively heterosexual (0). Five meant largely homosexual, but with incidental heterosexual history; four signified largely homosexual, but with distinct heterosexual history; three indicated equally heterosexual and homosexual; two meant largely heterosexual, but with a distinct homosexual history; and one signified largely heterosexual, but with incidental homosexual history.[1]

While this scale is helpful in clearing our minds of some of the misconceptions about homosexuality, it may in turn give rise to some misunderstandings of its own. It is doubtful whether the term homosexual should be applied to a person who has had casual contacts such as mutual masturbation in childhood or adolescence, or to a person isolated from heterosexual contacts, as in prison or like situations. It is certainly doubtful that a person, no matter how wayward his fantasy life, who has never been involved in any overt homosexual behavior should be called homosexual.

This large group of people is by no means homogeneous. They have only one thing in common—they have had some type of sexual interest in a person of their own sex. But the degree of interest, the type of behavior, and the commitment to homosexuality as a way of life varies greatly among these people.

There have probably been more false stereotypes concerning homosexuality than concerning any other type of human activity. Extreme forms range from the sissy, limp-wristed male, with his effeminate speech, to the solidly built woman in her mannish clothes, devoid of all soft feminine traits. These physical characteristics may be no indication at all of sexual orientation. A homosexual male may be strong and rugged in appearance, and the female (lesbian) soft, tender, and the essence of apparent femininity.

One of the tragedies of our day occurs when someone notes a man with effeminate characteristics or a woman with what may be interpreted as masculine traits and proceeds to circulate the story that this individual is gay. This labeling is cruel, unfair, and unchristian; and unless there is evidence of homosexual behavior or an open admission of such, no one has a right to make such an accusation.

Another group of people sometimes thought to be homosexuals are the *transvestites*. Transvestites are people who experience pleasure when clad in clothes of the opposite sex. Some studies indicate that as many as 96 percent of transvestites are heterosexuals. Another distinctive category is the *transsexual*; this classification includes those who wish to change their sex and who may have surgery to fulfill this desire.

I soon discovered that though they might be young or old, all of those in our group had an experience in common—they had "come out." To come out means to accept the fact that you are homosexual and to acknowledge this openly, seeking the company of other homosexuals. The person who hasn't come out has not faced himself. For years I had very brief contacts with other people. They didn't know me, nor I them. Now I had been discovered. I admitted to myself that I was a homosexual and then went on to acknowledge this openly to a group of people, many of whom were homosexuals.

I was over thirty years old before I knew anything about the gay world. From the time I was nineteen until I was thirty-one, I had been a loner. Now for the first time in my life I could let my hair down, I could be myself, and I could express my feelings without fear of being misunderstood or rejected. Psychology says that people who are not following the generally accepted mores of society feel much more comfortable when they are in the

*company of individuals with the same problems. This is
why homosexuals congregate in gay bars and other places.*

Probably the most heralded of all coming outs was that
of Sergeant Matlovich, who wrote a letter to his superior
officers in which he announced he was a homosexual.
When his startled superior asked, "What does this mean?"
the sergeant replied, "It means Brown versus the Board of
Education."

Matlovich referred to the court case which led to the
Supreme Court's striking down the idea of separate but
equal schools for blacks and whites. The court ordered
them to integrate "with all deliberate speed." Matlovich's
statement indicates that he saw his coming out as an event
that was going to give homosexuals a new status.

For most individuals, coming out takes place under
much more modest circumstances; and there's a good
chance it will happen in a gay bar.

*When my Mexican friend returned from San Francisco
to a nearby town, he invited me to visit him. I drove over
and he took me to a gay bar. It was the first time I had
been to one. From that time on, however, whenever I
was back in that town for the evening, I went to this place.
It gave me an opportunity to talk and have fun and make
a contact.*

*At the gay bar I drank wine. In my mind I had convinced
myself that wine and liquor were different; so while I refused
to have anything to do with hard liquor, I sat and sipped my*

*wine and smoked. Normally I didn't smoke; in fact, I
warned my young people against it. But I sat and smoked
to pass the time away, waiting to make a contact. A con-
venient way for someone to make a homosexual approach
is to say, "Do you have a light?" Particularly away from a
bar, but even in a bar, I would immediately realize that
this was an invitation for an encounter.*

*I was completely out of my normal character in this
setting. I never felt too guilty about drinking wine, but
my conscience bothered me because I had even gone to
the bar. I knew this was the wrong place for me to be.
Of course, most gay bars are filled with homosexuals.
Some men come in because they want to be picked up
by a homosexual. They go into the bar, let somebody
buy them a few beers, and then go out for a sexual encounter. Many of these men wouldn't normally engage
in homosexual activities, but alcohol is the great "superego
solvent"; and once it has done its work, conscience ceases
to be a bothersome reminder about values.*

*Some men go to gay bars to be picked up so that they
can get money. Although many would deny it, these hus-
tlers are actually male prostitutes.*

It has been estimated there are as many as four thousand
gay bars across the United States. One of these in Atlanta
has a capacity for some 1,100 people and is regularly filled.
The patrons are not all homosexuals, but most of them are.
These bars are the sexual marketplaces of the gays, where
they pick up partners and, in a short time, bring the brief

contact to an end before moving on to new prospects.

Once within the circles of the gay world, the new arrival begins to discover some peculiarities of this subculture.

When I became acquainted with this group, they introduced me to ideas and practices of the homosexual of which I wasn't even aware. Their talk was an absolute revelation to me. It is an esoteric language which is as difficult for the straight person to understand as a foreign tongue.

The man who had introduced me to the gay world only stayed around for a few months before he went to San Francisco, which has a notorious homosexual reputation. My wife opened one of his letters and read it. I was dead scared when I saw she had read it, but I need not have worried. His language was so veiled that she didn't understand what he was saying. He recounted an experience of spending the night at the YMCA. He had gone swimming where all the men were in the nude. Referring to himself, he said, "Your mother had a ball!" My wife innocently asked, "Does he know your mother?"

I am sure that the average person could be in a group where there were at least two homosexuals and not realize it. These two would soon become aware of each other. They could say things to each other and the straight people wouldn't have the faintest idea that they were carrying on a homosexual conversation.

One authority compiled a book called *The Queen's Vernacular,* a book of twelve thousand terms used in the gay world, but indicated that not all gays were excited about this special language and that activists among them see the gay slang as "another link in the chain that holds the homosexual enslaved."

Our discussion about the identity of the homosexual has led us into a number of areas and may have clouded rather than clarified the issues. It soon becomes obvious that a dictionary definition can be misleading. Homosexuality involves a type of sexual behavior; but this behavior leads to a whole way of life with a mystique of its own.

4. How Do People Become Homosexual?

"It is more correct to say that humans—and other mammals—have a capacity for heterosexual response and a capacity for homosexual response at birth, but that they do not have an inborn tendency toward either heterosexuality or homosexuality . . . ." From all evidence it becomes clear that the practice of homosexuality is learned behavior.

Homosexuality is the riddle of human sexual experiences. From the extent of the movement for gay liberation and the manner in which some are willing to be martyred for the cause, it becomes clear that the gay life-style is for many the quintessence of human sexual relations. On the other hand, for people with a normal heterosexual orientation who observe the simple facts of human anatomy and who accept as true the Bible verses "Male and female created he them" (Gen. 1:27) and "For this cause shall a man leave his father and mother and cleave unto his wife" (Gen. 2:24), the whole idea of people of the same sex being sexually involved with each other is not only inexplicable but perhaps completely repulsive.

Theories about the origin of homosexuality have occupied the minds of researchers for many years, and their conclusions have been speculative, fanciful, and on occasions almost ludicrous.

A commonly accepted explanation has been that sexual preference may have been inherited. In much the same way as red hair or some other physical characteristic is passed on from one generation to another, so some people inherit a homosexual nature, it is claimed. This theory hinges on the delicate hormonal balance within the individual.

This type of theorizing is extremely popular in the gay community. It means a man is no more responsible for his gayness than he is for his red hair or his Roman nose. Among the more religiously oriented, the argument picks up another dimension—"God made me this way, so that's the way I am— my homosexuality is the gift of God. I must come out and declare it and let everybody know my status."

In actual fact, there is virtually no scientific evidence to show that homosexuality is a part of an individual's genetic inheritance. One of the most exhaustive investigations ever made into human sexuality was carried on by Kinsey and his associates. Kinsey carefully examined the evidence and concluded, "There is no need of hypothesizing peculiar hormonal factors that make certain individuals especially liable to engage in homosexual activity, and we know of no data which prove the existence of such hormonal factors. There are no sufficient data indicating that specific hereditary factors are involved." [1]

Another group of psychologists looks to the relationship of a child to his or her parents, generally of the opposite sex, as the explanation for the development of homosexuality. There might be a weak or objectionable father; the boy "falls in love" with his mother and is scared by his incestuous ideas, which now affect all his sexual attitudes toward women. Similar ideas give rise to theories about the child's falling in love with the parent of his own sex and then desiring to be a sexual partner for the loved parent.

There is probably no area of study involving homosexual behavior where speculation has been more poetic, picturesque, and less convincing than the parent-child relationships explanation.

Another theory focuses on the development within the growing personality. Human development is a complex process; and as far as his love life is concerned, the individual faces a series of love objects—self, mother, father, playmates of one's own sex, someone of the opposite sex, the spouse, children, grandchildren, and finally humanity. The process moves in ever-widening circles reaching out from self to humanity.

Human personality is relatively fluid and subject to interruptions and diversions in the developmental processes. Two roadblocks to development are the psychological mechanism of fixation and regression.

In the later days of his life, Robert Louis Stevenson, the famous author, went to Samoa in pursuit of good health. There he built a house on an elevated spot overlooking the sea. He endeared himself to the natives by his acts of kindness and interest in their affairs. When he was restricted in his movements by sickness, the natives showed their gratitude by building a road from his house right down the mountainside. It was called the Road of the Loving Heart. There is a sense in which every individual must climb the road of the loving heart; but like a climber who might reach a point in the climb and decide to go no further, we may be *fixated*. The climber may turn around and retreat. In this way we can *regress* to an early love object, canceling out normal development patterns.

Investigators claim that before age fifteen some 33 percent of girls and 60 percent of boys engage in some type of homosexual experimentation. These are generally fumbling efforts at understanding sexuality and do not indicate homosexual tendencies. Within the context of the maturation process, this type of behavior is normal.

From about age fifteen onward there is a natural movement toward heterosexual experiences. Adolescence is a
time of adjustment; and, with the advent of puberty, the
adolescent experiences a hormonal surge causing rapid
growth of the primary and secondary sexual characteristics. Pubic hair, sex organs, and the developing body get
much attention.

During this time of an emerging, sometimes throbbing sexuality, the adolescent may be more self-conscious, more un-
certain and anxious. Because of this factor, a group of
peers frequently provides a safe milieu for sexual talk,
comparison of sex organs, and sexual experimentation.

The boy, vividly aware of his own sexuality, moves toward the female as a desirable sex object in the anticipa-
tion that she will respond to his approaches. He discovers
that her sexual requirements are not nearly as direct as his
and that her developing sexuality manifests itself in a demand for attention and continuing pursuit in return for
the smallest favors. At this time a boy frequently accepts
the comfortable experimentation with members of his own
sex as second best, but as bringing relief from sexual
pressures.

*The adult homosexual often finds something attractive
about younger partners. They always appealed to me, and
a teenage boy looked particularly attractive. I have noticed,
too, that some magazines which cater to homosexuals feature
pictures of nude boys as young as ten or eleven.*

From the boy's perspective there is the subtle implication

from authority figures that, although sexual relations with females are forbidden, what boys do with other males may be quite all right. As the mature male homosexual approaches the adolescent, he skillfully initiates him into a world of sexuality. In addition to this, he may reward the adolescent for participating. When the adolescent attempts to relate to a female, he becomes vividly aware of all the difficulties of heterosexual experience. Memories of his earlier homosexual encounters may persistently lure him back.

Perhaps Kinsey Was Right

Add to these developmental factors yet another consideration, and much of the mystery disappears. The complex process of learning gives us a simple explanation of the manner in which homosexuality is a learned behavior.

Examine any writings on human sexuality, and you will certainly find some reference to the Kinsey report. Most of the quotes from his monumental work are generally used against traditional interpretation of standards of sexual behavior. Well, if Kinsey is so good, why not pay some attention to his statement about the origin of inversion?

Kinsey, after rejecting the ideas of heredity, hormones, and parental relations, says that there are four factors that must be considered in accounting for homosexuality. These are: "(1) The basic physiologic capacity of every mammal to respond to any sufficient stimulus; (2) the accident which leads an individual into his or her first sexual experience with a person of the same sex; (3) the conditioning effects of such experience; and (4) the indirect but powerful conditioning which the opinions of other persons and the social codes may have on an individual's decision to accept or reject this type of sexual contact."[2]

After a long period of time in which any events in life had to be accounted for in terms of indistinctive forces, many psychologists are turning to a closer examination of behavior—how it is learned and supported by its consequences. The primitive sex drive is an inner force with a tremendous potential variety in its expression as seen in the many varieties of sexual activity which people come to like and demand.

The Oneida perfectionists provide us with an excellent example of the possible expressions of the sex drive. Philip Humphrey Noyes founded this community-living project and, as part of its activities, set up a type of birth control to make sure that children were only born of selected parents. To accomplish this aim the men were taught the art of "male continence," technically known as *coitus reservatus.* Although a rather difficult sexual feat, the technique was learned by the men of the community and came to be viewed by them as a highly prized sexual experience. It was undoubtedly anything but normal.

Those who work with behavior modification have shown how behaviors can be established and, once the powers of habit take over, can continue on. We have noticed Kinsey's ideas about the development of homosexual reactions, particularly the statement, "(2) the accident which leads the individual into his or her first sexual experience with a person of the same sex; (3) the conditioning effects of this experience." [3] Evidence turned up by other researchers corroborates Kinsey's conclusions.

The Kinseys of our day are Masters and Johnson, who

have approached the whole matter of sexual research from a more clinical angle. Their work produced a similar conclusion about homosexuality. Of 213 men whom they treated for sexual dysfunction, 21 had homosexual experiences as teenagers. Apparently the first initiatory sexual encounter was a significant factor. None of these men had engaged in heterosexual encounters before their homosexual activity. The conclusion was, "The man whose first mature sexual experience is homosexual appears to be marked by it, even though he switches to heterosexual lovemaking. There may be some pattern imprinted on his behavior that cannot be erased. Both primarily and secondarily impotent men who had homosexual experiences as teenagers continued to think of themselves as homosexually oriented in their adult lives, even though many married." [4]

Another researcher investigated the question about whether homosexual desires or homosexual behavior came first. The investigator discovered that in a significant number of cases he looked into, his subjects had their first homosexual experiences before they were conscious of any homosexual desires. Another 12.3 percent of his subjects developed homosexual desires and homosexual behavior at about the same time. Significantly, in all the cases investigated by this researcher, 43 percent of the subjects had their first homosexual experiences before they were twelve years old. [5]

One researcher of the phenomenon of group sex discovered that homosexual activities between females are often a feature of these events. The lesbian activities were introduced at the command of the men, and investigation showed that two-thirds of the women who participated learned to enjoy lesbian activities. Some of them even went on to function exclusively as lesbians. Urged on by their male tutors, they had learned the lesson—learned it only too well—with the result that they turned aside from males who had used them badly, exploiting their lesbian activities for their own satisfaction, and had now become lesbians in the fullest sense of the word.

Wainwright Churchill's investigation of homosexuality led him into many paths as he studied the sexual behavior of many cultures—Greek and Roman, ancient tribal and modern primitive, northern and southern, European and American, as well as nonhuman species. He finally concluded about the origin of homosexuality, "It is more correct to say that humans—and other mammals—have a capacity for heterosexual response and a capacity for homosexual response at birth, but that they do not have an inborn tendency toward either heterosexuality or homosexuality. After the drive has been conditioned one way or the other or both ways—in other words, after the capacity for response has been exploited and learning has begun—we may speak of a tendency toward heterosexuality and/or a tendency toward homosexuality. But this tendency is acquired and is a product of learning rather than a part of the individual's biological inheritance. To speak of a tendency toward heterosexuality or homosexuality that is independent of learning is simply to invent a new vocabulary for the old concept of instinct." [6]

From all evidence it becomes clear that the practice of homosexuality is learned behavior. The use of the word *learned* may create some confusion, for it generally suggests that the subject has deliberately set himself an objective and that, by arduous concentration, he has gained the skills and knowledge in question. What actually happens is that most learning takes place unwittingly, without the awareness of the individual that anything is happening. As certain experiences have pleasant consequences, they are repeated without conscious effort, while experiences without pleasant consequences may be unwittingly abandoned. Skillful teachers teach a lesson without the awareness of the student.

Conditioning is a word used to describe the way in which a learning experience can be arranged, sometimes without either teacher or learner realizing what is happening. If you came into my house I would introduce you to my French poodle, Max; and just to break the ice I'd have him "do his thing."

I walk to the table and make a scratching noise on the tabletop; and Max immediately stands up on his hind legs, does a cute little dance, and makes doggy noises. There's a distinct possibility that you'll courteously murmur that Max is "clever." As a matter of fact, he's not really clever—he's dumb. Max doesn't know why he performs his act, but I know the reason.

One day a visitor came to our home with a cardboard box containing three horned toads. The curious poodle ran over to greet the visitor, who responded by opening the box and lowering it for Max to see the strange little reptiles. Max—who has had a very limited experience in life—became excited at the sight of these frightened little creatures pushing away from him in the box. Then the visitor took the box and placed it on a low table. Max immediately, like some army sentry placed on duty, sat with his eyes riveted on the box. Periodically the horned toads would scratch around, and whenever they did Max would jump up on his hind legs to peep at them.

Now every time Max hears a scratching noise on the table,

he springs up on his hind legs. Some people would say
he's been conditioned. Whenever he stood on his hind
legs and looked into the box, he was rewarded with the
view of the horned toads. Max has learned a lesson without being aware of it. Now he has a harmless built-in
routine for life.

But what about the teaching and learning factors in
homosexuality? In the years of childhood and early
adolescence the human is in a situation where sexuality
is particularly pliable. Add to this the penchant of homosexuals to turn to younger sex objects, and we are confronted with the heart of the problem. If gays are entitled to their own sexual preferences, should not each
individual have the same privilege? Biologically the child
is being prepared for heterosexual functioning—does anyone have the right to condition him into the imprisonment
of homosexual reaction?

5. Woman to Woman

When Queen Victoria was asked to sign the Criminal Law Amendment of 1885, a piece of legislation that made homosexual acts between adults illegal, she refused to put her signature to the document until all references to women were removed. The queen made it clear that, in her opinion, no such relationships existed. Her Majesty would have been astounded had she been able to look into the future and see that her change of law would give lesbians protection from prosecution in Great Britain.

Stella is a lesbian who is going through a time of reevaluation. Here she freely talks about her feelings.

We were laughing and cutting up, and then I said something particularly cute. She grinned real big and leaned forward and kissed me on the lips. It was a passionate kiss, and I responded. Well, I didn't know what had hit me; and she looked very surprised herself. We tried to discuss what had happened, but how do you discuss a thing like that? A few nights later she came by to get me to go for a drive to discuss what had happened, and we ended up in a parked car kissing. It is especially important to realize here just how very much we loved each other! Physical expression seemed like a natural expression of the love which was overflowing in both of us.

I don't think it ever really dawned on me at this time that the relationship would go any further than kissing. I had no reason to think that it would. [Chalk up another point for learned behavior.] As I think back on what my feelings were at this time, I recall guilt and excitement battling one

*another, only to be outdone by confusion. I like to think
of myself as the young innocent child who was taken advantage of, but there's no use trying to kid myself. I could
have said no at any time.*

*Another significant fact that I have accepted only lately
is that I had to do something somewhere along the line to
let Eleanor know for sure that her affections would not be
rejected. I don't think I was aware of this as I was innocently
being warm and loving. Little did I realize that I was laying
the foundation for our relationship. As we began to see
each other more and more, our physical involvement grew.*

In many ways Queen Victoria was the quintessence of a
straitlaced morality. She has left her name as a symbol of
a starchy, puritanical attitude toward human sexuality.
When Queen Victoria was asked to sign the Criminal Law
Amendment of 1885, a piece of legislation that made homosexual acts between adults illegal, she refused to put her
signature to the document until all references to women
were removed. The queen made it clear to all that, in her
opinion, no such relationships existed. Her Majesty would
have been astounded had she been able to look into the
future and see that her change of law would give lesbians
protection from prosecution in Great Britain.

Queen Victoria's blissful ignorance about lesbianism may
be typical of what is going on in churches today. Many
church members feel they don't really need to know what
is happening in the sinful world around them. Male homosexuality is a repugnant enough subject—but when someone
begins to talk about female homosexuality, they, like Queen

Victoria, prefer to believe that it does not exist or at least that what you don't know won't hurt you.

The word *lesbian,* now widely used for female homosexuality, has a fascinating background. It comes from the name of the Greek island of Lesbos, where lived a famous poet of antiquity named Sappho (a word meaning clear voiced or bright). It is claimed that she was of royal birth and that her influence was such that she easily gathered a circle of young girls around her in a school that became famous for its cultivation of poetry, music, dancing, and the glorification of women's love for women. Of her it was said, "Sappho's life and poetry are filled with the love of her own sex."

With lesbians, as with male homosexuals, there are many misunderstandings. The popular stereotype of the lesbian is of a female completely unfeminine, a sort of male in a female body. This is not necessarily so. In fact, the traits we generally associate with feminity, such as gentleness and kindness, may be the very factors that could cause a girl to move into lesbianism as she reacts to the harshness and crudity of the male who makes coarse, aggressive sexual overtures to her. Within lesbian ranks, many terms are used; but two, *butch* and *femme*, are broad categories frequently utilized. The word *butch* describes the active, aggressive female, very frequently masculine in dress and attitude, while *femme* describes the more feminine passive female homosexual.

After having gone to all this trouble to make the distinction between butch and femme, we should note that many lesbians would not agree. One very prominent activist in the lesbian movement was described in this way by her interviewer: "A tall figure with scraggly long hair and a

bulky dungaree jacket. She pulls nervously on the lapels of
her denim jacket, and I try not to stare at red stars and
multicolored insignia embroidered on it. A loose-fitting
man's shirt does not hide her outlines. As she stands to get
another drink, I see her cartoony, huge, laced-up floppy
mountain boots. She carries an Army khaki pack with a
mermaid sewed on it as a handbag." This person herself
states her case: "The old butch-femme distinction—passive
or aggressive homosexual—is ridiculous. Like most lesbians,
I'm happily confused. I'm intellectually aggressive—and
aggressive as an athlete and a dancer—but sexually most
women are passive. I guess when I find somebody I really
like I become more aggressive." [1]

While there is a tendency to gather all homosexuals,
male and female, under one broad heading and say, "All
homosexuals are this or that way," in actual experience
there are a number of distinctions that should be made.
Preeminent among these are the differences between the
masculine and feminine homosexuality. This difference
will be a continuing theme throughout the chapter, but
some of the more obvious distinctions are:

(1) Many of the earlier understandings of homosexuality
indicated that it is an experience in which two males engage in sodomy and fellatio, the former being specifically
forbidden in the Bible and the latter a repulsive idea to
many people. In lesbianism the activity of sodomy would
be an impossibility, and little is known by the general public
about lesbian cunnilingus. Consequently, lesbianism appeared
on the surface to be much more soft and gentle than the
coarser masculine homosexuality; and for many years the
term was only whispered.

(2) The biblical idea of human sexuality had its basis in the fact that sexuality was designed by a wise Creator for the process of reproduction. Onan's sin was a case in point. The condemnation was not of masturbation but rather that the semen which should have been used to reproduce life was wasted. The same idea was prominent in Catholic teachings. In lesbian relationships no such loss of semen was involved, causing it to be looked upon differently from masculine homosexual practices where the semen was "wasted."

(3) Society as a whole has been much more tolerant of a relationship between two women than it has of one between men. As a boy I remember two adolescent girls who spent much time hugging and kissing, sitting on the front porch, as did lovers in that day. Nobody bothered too much about this relationship; but if two boys had participated in the same activities, there would have been real trouble.

(4) Prostitution is always a disruptive factor in society and degrades the use of human sexuality. While there is a considerable amount of prostitution among male homosexuals, the practice is virtually unknown among lesbians. This seamier side of exploitive sexuality is not as obvious a feature of lesbianism, which is consequently not as abhorrent to many people.

(5) Part of the attitude of tolerance towards lesbians as opposed to male homosexuals may come from the rather condescending masculine attitude that some unfortunate women don't have what it takes to attract a male, so they settle for second best in seeking sexual—social relationships with a woman.

(6) In an extension of the idea of masculine ownership of all types of goods, among which would be a wife, few men feel threatened by the sight of two women making love. On the other hand, a great proportion of men would receive no satisfaction from the sight of two males involved in sexual activity. This is clearly seen in the so-called "swinging" activities or group sex, from which come reports of men urging women to engage in lesbian activities; but masculine homosexual behavior to them is taboo and ordinarily is not practiced in these groups.

(7) Another factor is the perfectly justifiable fear people have of the use of force in sex. Most people have the idea that certain male homosexuals are child molesters and rapists, but lesbians are thought of more as feminine, soft, and unlikely to resort to force.

From these considerations it becomes clear that we cannot speak about homosexuality as an activity easily definable and describable. And the major distinction will be between male homosexuality and lesbianism. As our discussion proceeds, each of these distinctions will serve to show lesbianism as a distinctive entity.

Lesbianism may have wider implications than we sometimes think. It has only been in comparatively recent days that lesbians have become so militant, and this aggressiveness has been fanned to a flame by two new activist enterprises in our society. One of these is the new aggressive gay movement of male homosexuals, who are insisting on their rights. Lesbians feel that they are in the same dilemma as the male homosexuals and want the right of making their own sex object choices; but they find that the gay move-

ment is male dominated and doesn't provide a good vehicle
for their aspirations. Very naturally, lesbians have turned
to a second protest movement in our society and have
sought a place in the burgeoning feminist movements—only
to discover that many of the feminists, while anxious to
make new gains for women, are not sure they want to take
on the added burden of championing a crusade for homosexuality.

Among lesbians, there are few self-doubts about their
cause. They see themselves as the standard bearers of the
women's rights organization. As an article in *Time* noted,
"Some of the more radical feminists insisted that lesbianism
is the only logical answer to women's oppression and accused
heterosexual feminists of collusion with the enemy." One
of the most vocal of this group says, "Feminism at heart is
a massive complaint. Lesbianism is the solution." [2]

This feminist attitude toward males is another in the long
list of distinctives between the male homosexual and the
lesbian. While many male homosexuals may enjoy the company of women and apparently make good companions
and friends for their female acquaintances, the lesbian movement is antimale. In an article entitled "The Bulldozer
Rapist," a lesbian tells at length about a bulldozer operator
doing some work around her house and about his crude sexual approaches. She concludes, "It's the Bulldozer Rapist
concept of masculinity, a concept shared to one degree or
another by most of the male population, that leads women
to choose a lesbian life-style. Lesbianism is a flight from association with or dependency on the masculine. Masculinity as I see it is rude and ugly and at the root of most of the
world's problems." [3] This antimale attitude makes lesbians
the shock troops of the women's lib movement and will be

a perpetual barrier to the formation of a healthy family union between male and female.

Yet another of the distinctives of lesbianism is seen in the place of relationship in the experience. Lesbians tend to think in terms of relationship rather than focusing on the orgasmic moment, which characterizes much masculine homosexuality. The Kinsey study, for example, showed a high proportion of lesbians, 51 percent, who had their homosexual experience with just one person; another 20 percent had it with two partners; 25 percent had three partners; while only 4 percent had more than ten partners. By way of contrast, the male homosexuals had a tendency toward promiscuity, with some 22 percent having their experiences with ten or more partners. Some respondents reported their number of partners to be in the hundreds. [4]

Small wonder lesbians complain when they are just lumped in with the male homosexuals. They protest that males who comment on lesbians cannot get beyond genital contacts, which apparently have some attraction for the male mind. Lesbians urge outsiders to give more consideration to the friendship aspect of their situation.

What effect did this relationship have on other relationships in my life during the past three years? It has caused me to fear emotional involvement with women. I can think of five friends with whom I allowed myself to become emotionally involved, and all five times—because of my past experience—it almost seemed to be a natural response of my love for them to express myself physically. Because I did not know how to cope with my feelings, I usually pulled away from the relationships. I never thought of myself as lesbian, but I knew that my feelings were not normal; and I found myself blaming them on Eleanor.

I once officiated at a wedding of a man and woman who were already married. They were both Dutch citizens; and he, while living in Australia, had proposed to his girlfriend, at that time a resident in Holland. They had then married by proxy. Immediately upon arrival in Australia, the little Dutch girl insisted on a religious ceremony, so they were married the second time.

But a "couple" in Boulder, Colorado, went one better when they married three times—first in the college dormitory, then in a religious ceremony, and finally, in the office of the Boulder County Clerk. They have now set up a joint checking account, arranged the deductions on their paychecks, and taken a new name which is a hyphenated combination of their two premarriage names.

What makes this marriage different is that the principals in this new union are Sophie and Matilda, two lesbians who have taken advantage of the county clerk's ruling that under Colorado law, same-sex marriages are *not illegal.* It should be noted that not all the citizenry of that city were delighted at the news, and one cowboy in protest tried to marry his horse.

This effort at legalizing a marriage is another indication of lesbian desire for relationship and commitment. The very desire for such a relationship may become the Achilles' heel of lesbian liaisons, for it inspires a strong reaction of jealousy. In chapter 7 I have reported several cases in which I have been involved and was amazed at the intensity of a jealousy which led lesbians to do horrible things to each other. These situations may confirm psychological findings that lesbian relationships are characterized by hostility.

At one gathering in which I found myself confronted with a whole group of lesbians, I was amazed at their intensity. When I tried to get the discussion onto a nonemotional basis, one asked, "You stated that lesbian relationships seem to be characterized by jealousy, but isn't it true that many heterosexual relationships pass through stages when one is jealous of the other?" My answer to this is that yes, jealousy is a component of many heterosexual relationships; however, if it occurs to any degree of intensity in any relationship, it is generally pathological and, from my perspective, indicative of an underlying guilt.

By my junior year in college our once-beautiful relationship was quite lacking. The old song "All or Nothing At All" seemed to apply to us. I am almost certain that I could have had a warm and loving relationship without the physical. Eleanor could not. Therefore, many times we acted like perfect strangers. I hated it—the pretending that we didn't care when we really did. Because we lived in the same town, attended the same church, and were involved in many of the same activities, we were constantly being thrown together. She tried very hard to get me out of her system, and many times I was almost convinced that she didn't care anymore and was very hurt.

You might say that I wanted to "have my cake and eat it too." I did not want her to love me any less, but I did want a changed relationship. My back-and-forth attitude caused her much pain. Just as she would really begin to stand strong and be on top of her feelings and emotions, I would always come on strong just to make sure that she

*really hadn't gotten me out of her system . . . then I
would be on my way again. I enjoyed knowing that our
relationship depended on what I wanted it to be; I liked
being in control.*

The Bible has little to say about lesbianism, but there
is one very clear statement in the Roman epistle where
Paul said, "Their women exchanged natural relations for
unnatural" (Rom. 1:26, RSV). While most unbiased readers
see "natural" as heterosexual relationships, the lesbian has
another point of view.

In a panel discussion on "When Women Love Other
Women," a lesbian addressed herself to the question of
the development of homosexuality in terms of "What went
wrong?" Her response was, "I feel this is a mistake. It is
like saying the natural thing is for everyone to be right-
handed, so we will investigate the minority position of
left-handness. You would come up with some pretty distorted information in that way. The underlying assump-
tion that something has gone wrong to cause homosexuality is, it seems to me, suspect." [5] The reference to right-
handedness is typical of the argument which says, "I was
born this way. I can't help it. If God made me this way,
it would be unnatural for me not to be a homosexual."

This is the favorite argument of homosexuality. It
is an extension of the difficulty we face with people whose
lives fall into an unmanageable mess. There is generally a
shrugging of the shoulders ("I couldn't help it" or "Why
did this happen to me?"). So the homosexual claims, "I
can't help it; it's the way I was born." In chapter 4 we
noted some of the evidence that homosexuality is a learned

activity. Any process of learning calls for some participation on the part of the learner; it is not that easy to duck responsibility. One very successful skill of psychotherapy maintains that all so-called "mental illness" is really irresponsibility and that the way back to meaningful living is to start by accepting at least some responsibility. The argument "I am made this way" may really be a cop-out.

The mentioning of the word natural and associating it with the creative work of God raises an important issue that involves creation and the manner in which the all-wise Creator made our bodies. Dr. Reuben states a major problem of lesbian lovemaking, which is that of having only half the pieces in the anatomical jigsaw puzzle. [6] Lesbian sexual activities include kissing, masturbation, generalized body contact, caressing, cunnilingus, and tribadism. Taking into consideration the anatomical structure of male and female, it is very difficult to speak about "natural" and at the same time to invoke the name of God as Creator who made people like this. Every evidence of human bodies that comes from the hands of this Creator indicates his great plan that male and female should become "one flesh." The comment of one person may be appropriate here: "Basically all homosexuals are alike—looking for love when there can be no love and looking for sexual satisfaction where there can be no lasting satisfaction." [7]

Male homosexuals and lesbians alike have a tendency to interpret any statement about the shortcomings of homosexuality as an attack upon a gentle people. This reaction is somewhat akin to the repressive government which attacks conscientious objectors in their society. So it is common practice to refer to expositions of homosexuality as being full of hatred. Yet in the flood of literature presently available, there is a strange lack of material about disadvantages of lesbianism. Most of it pours out the hate message against straights.

This fact is clearly seen in one publication in which Christianity becomes a target. "According to the Judeo-Christian, women are less important than men: they are, in fact, as the language of the quoted passage (Rom. 1:26) makes clear, the property of men: their women." [8] Psychology is a target. "Even psychology is traditionally the enemy of women." [9] The church? "The church—the institution, its doctrine, its believers—has expressed its woman hatred, its lesbian hatred, in a number of ways." [10] Society itself is viewed as an enemy in which lesbianism is "thus in rebellion against a woman-hating society." [11] And having protested for many years against the use of the word *perversion,* a spokeswoman for lesbianism declares, "Exclusive heterosexuality has to be understood as a *perversion* of this natural state." [12] Even the dreaded label of "unnatural" is not too serious to apply to straights: "It is not the Lesbian or the Gay man who is unnatural but rather the heterosexual person." [13] From an examination of these statements it is not necessarily the straights who are cruel, unkind, and full of hatred, but the aggressive lesbians.

It may be that the major message of lesbianism is the danger of the use of force in sex. It is somewhat ironic that in urging fewer restraints on sexual expression, lesbians may be helping to unleash the torrent of pornography that has flooded our land today. One of the major indictments of the muck merchants is that in their desire to titillate, they have distorted human sexuality and miseducated many people. Because it is necessary to go to extremes to titillate the portrayal of sexual activity, they have become more crude in portraying sadistic practices as the ultimate in sexual experiences. Many of these depictions are of women who rejoice in being raped and tortured. In actual fact, most women want above everything else kindness, gentleness, and patience in lovemaking.

Christian parents may face a particularly difficult situation in rearing their children. Anxious that a daughter should not violate her Christian moral standards and aware of the possibilities of out-of-wedlock sexual activity, parents will warn her against sexual overtures from boys. One counselor reported the case of a counselee who had developed a relationship with her female teacher. "My parents warned me against boys. But they never said anything about girls, and I never thought there was anything wrong with my relationship with my teacher—until later."

A wise Christian parent needs to discuss the creative aspect of human sexuality and the goodness of sex but to point out that, like so many good gifts, it can easily be misused. A girl can be exploited by some male whose sexual interests are much more directly genital than hers. But the existence of exploitive use of sex by some males should not blind her to the wonderful place of sex as a fulfilling experience within a marriage commitment, when a husband and wife become "one flesh." It would also be wise to point out that there is an emotional exploitation which might be more devastating when a lesbian relationship runs its course.

Lesbianism and marriage are incompatible. A fairly typical pattern is the girl who married young, then later begins to wonder. Her husband seems to lack ambition, and she feels that she has not achieved her potential. She decides to go back to college and, in the environment of the college, discovers bright-eyed girls her own age. They feed her the typical lesbian line—men are exploiters of women; they are coarse and cruel in their sexual demands. All of this propaganda is contrasted with the tender affection of the new female friends: "We understand and share your ambitions; none of us would ever be demanding of you; our love is gentle and kind." The crowning argument may be, "You have tried the heterosexual way; you can contrast the superiority of lesbian love."

The married lesbian puts herself into the driver's seat. While her husband is at work, she can enjoy her lesbian relationships. When her husband suggests lovemaking she is able to cut him down to size by using such terms as "oversexed" and by keeping him in a constant state of frustration. The wife who is aware that, if her lesbianism is known, she will not get custody of the children, has only one course open to her; she stays in the marriage, which remains in a constant state of tension. Because of the antimale attitude, marriage to a lesbian may be even worse than a marriage involving male homosexuality.

The family is God's institution and would be nonexistent without loving men and women. The relationship of male and female is the raw material out of which so much of the zest of life is made. Some people may elect to live the single life, and that is a legitimate choice and their own business; but when a movement becomes antimale it is a mockery of what God has laid down as his plan.

On television there suddenly appeared a remarkable program titled *The Incredible Machine.* A presentation from the National Geographic Society, it showed how a human body (two-thirds water, the rest nitrogen, carbon calcium, and a myriad of other chemicals worth only about five dollars at today's inflated prices) is nevertheless amazing in its functioning. Nowhere was this more dramatically indicated than in a demonstration of two pieces of tissue from the heart muscle, lying in a culture dish. Though separated from the rest of the heart tissue, each piece continued to pulsate at a distinctive individual rhythm. Then the experimenter pushed the two pieces into contact with each other. Once the two pieces of tissue made contact, each immediately abandoned its individual rhythm; and the two beat in unison. Husbands and wives are like this. Each has his or her own unique rhythm of life, but in marriage the two learn to live by a distinctive, interacting rhythm.

Lesbianism has a certain longing note. One woman reporter tells of going to a gathering of lesbians and describes an insightful incident. "One woman with a kind smile, long curly hair, and a lot of rings noticed me writing in my notebook. She asked if I was gay or straight. When I said I was straight, she said wistfully, 'You're lucky.' "

6. What Does the Bible Teach About Homosexuality?

The command of God is for men and women to be fruitful and multiply . . . . Consequently, human sexuality is not dirty or unclean or sinful. It may be one of the most important functions that a human being fulfills. Men and women can take pride in the fact that God has invited them to join with him in his creative activity . . . . On the other hand, deviant sexuality is condemned. There are a number of passages in the Bible where homosexuality is specifically mentioned.

The Bible says a lot about homosexuality. In fact, it has much to say on the general topic of human sexuality.

The command of God is for men and women to be fruitful and multiply. In the creation story we are told that God created heaven and earth and saw that almost everything was good. As he looked around he saw one thing that was not good: "It is not good that man should be alone" (Gen. 2:18). So God gave the commandment to be fruitful and multiply. Consequently, human sexuality is not dirty or unclean or sinful. It may be one of the most important functions that a human being fulfills. Men and women can take pride in the fact that God has invited them to join with him in his creative activity.

In addition to being creative, sex is also pleasurable; and the Bible also speaks about pleasurable sexual experiences. The Song of Solomon, a book long dear to the hearts of mystical Christians, is really a love song. So we find the statement:

BRIDEGROOM: You stand there straight as a palm,
                        with breasts like clusters of fruit;
                  methinks I will climb that palm,

taking hold of the boughs!
Oh may your breasts be clusters of fruit,
    and your breath sweet as an apple!

BRIDE: I am my darling's and he—
    he is longing for me.
Come away to the fields, O my darling,
    and let us sleep in the blossoms of henna,
and hie us at dawn to the vineyards,
    to see if the vines are a-budding,
if their blossoms are open,
    if pomegranates bloom;
and there I will give you caresses of love
    (Song of Sol. 7:7-12, Moffatt).

Many a reader of the book of Proverbs is surprised to discover the type of problems under discussion. Prominent among these is human sexuality. The book abounds with warnings to young people about sexual temptation and the dangers of illicit sexuality. When it comes to combating temptation, Proverbs presents an interesting technique: "Let your manhood be a blessing; rejoice in the wife of your youth. Let her charms and tender embrace [breasts] satisfy you. Let her love alone fill you with delight" (Prov. 5:18-19, TLB).

On the other hand, deviant sexuality is condemned. There are a number of passages in the Bible where homosexuality is specifically mentioned.

Some clergymen tend to minimize what the Bible says about homosexuality. Their main argument seems to be that the Jewish people were opposed to homosexuality because it would slow down the processes of reproduction, which were important to a primitive people badly needing population. In modern times, since we have a population explosion, this is no longer a valid criticism. Having disposed of the Old Testament argument that Paul was Jewish and carried over these ideas into the New Testament, therefore, an intelligent modern Christian doesn't have to accept these prohibitions.

This argument doesn't appeal to me. On this basis it might be possible to wriggle out of almost any biblical prohibition. All my life I have belonged to what might be called conservative churches, where we felt the Bible gave us a pretty good basis for personal conduct. When I began to examine the biblical teachings about homosexuality, my conscience found little comfort.

I have often heard people in favor of more permissive attitudes toward homosexuality plead for a more "Christian" approach. Yet a reading of the New Testament indicates that Christianity in its early days was characterized by an uncompromising hostility toward homosexual practices.

I became convinced of the Bible's antipathy to the secret practices of my life. In the grip of a tortured conscience I discovered just how troublesome a well-formed value system can be. I contemplated suicide and frequently asked God to take my life.

The Drama of Sodom

Of the twelve passages in the Bible which refer implicitly

or explicitly to homosexuality, the first and for many the most declarative denunciation of the practice is the passage that tells of the destruction of Sodom and Gomorrah. Abraham had pleaded with God to save the city if he could find as few as ten righteous men. God sent two messengers, angels dressed as men, to carry out the search. These two men stayed the night with Lot; and the inhabitants of the city, hearing about them surrounded the house and demanded: "Where are the men which came into thee this night? bring them out to us, that we may know them" (Gen. 19:5).

The explanation offered by homosexuals who want to water down this statement is that the Hebrew word translated *know* could be used to mean "get acquainted with." As they see it, the desire of the Sodomites was to interrogate the two visitors and find out if they were spies. They probably had no thought of sexual activity.

The Hebrew language does have a limited number of words; consequently, one word can be used in many ways, as is true of our own English language. However, this Hebrew word *yadha* is used in Genesis to describe the sexual relations between Adam and his wife. In situations like this the context of the verse is important. If the men of Sodom only desired to meet Lot's visitors, why did Lot offer them his daughters? Lot clearly felt that the men of Sodom wanted to know the visitors in the same way that he offered them the possibility of knowing his daughters.

Other translations by Hebrew scholars highlight the same idea: "Where are the men who came to visit you tonight? Bring them out to us that we may rape them" (Gen. 19:5, Moffatt). "Bring out those men to us so we may rape them" (Gen. 19:5, TLB). Confirmation of the nature of the activity in Sodom is found in the epistle of Jude: "Even as Sodom and Gomorrah, and the cities about them in like manner, giving themselves over to fornication, and going after strange flesh, are set forth for an example, suffering the vengeance of eternal fire" (v. 7).

This passage obviously indicates that the homosexual experience is not new and that it was typically carried on in the depraved city that fell under the judgment of God.

The Levitical Commands

The book of Leviticus has been called the "spiritual statute book" of Israel. Here were laid down the principles to help the Israelites become the people that God wanted them to be. The book not only speaks of the holiness of God and the manner in which his people are to approach him, but also gives practical commands as to how they are to behave.

The book contains two statements about homosexuality. The first says:

> Thou shalt not lie with mankind, as with womankind: it is abomination (Lev. 18:22).

The second passage states:

> If a man also lie with mankind, as he lieth with a woman, both of them have committed an abomination: they shall surely be put to death; their blood shall be upon them (Lev. 20:13).

The homosexual argument against paying much attention

to these statements is that the Jews desperately needed a bigger population. God had commanded his people to "be fruitful and multiply" (Gen. 1:28), and the promise to Abraham was that his descendants would be as numerous as the sands of the sea. In the same vein, the aim of these statements was to discourage any activity that might slow down population growth. The gay argument holds that today we face a population explosion and that homosexuality may be the answer to the problem—therefore, the biblical command is of no importance.

The answer to this position is that in this Scripture there is a penalty for homosexuality—the penalty is death. This is infinitely more serious than something that would come upon people who failed to reproduce. It is the condemnation of a practice offensive to God.

The attitude of homosexuals toward the Levitical code is seen in an interchange between Troy Perry, a homosexual minister, and a Los Angeles pedestrian. He has just given a woman a gay tract, and she has attacked him with her purse.

> She looked me over, backed off a step, and I thought she was going to hit me again. She said, "Young man, do you know what the book of Leviticus says?"
>
> I told her, "I sure do! It says that it's a sin for a woman to wear a red dress. for a man to wear a cotton shirt and woolen pants at the same time, for anyone to eat shrimp, oysters, or lobster—or your steak too rare."
>
> She said, "That's not what I mean!"
>
> I said, "I know that's not what you mean, Honey, but you forgot all of these other dreadful sins, too, that are in the same book of the Bible." [1]

Perry, of course, is overlooking the fact that Christians

are no longer under the Levitical law as far as sacrifices and similar practices are concerned. On the other hand, the condemnation of homosexuality is not only found in Leviticus; it is a continuing note in both the Old and New Testaments.

The Roman Situation

The courts of the Roman Empire were notorious for their corruption, and Paul spelled out the situation very clearly in the first chapter of Romans. As he wrote about the characteristics of Roman depravity, he mentioned homosexuality.

> For this cause God gave them up unto vile affections: for even their women did change the natural use into that which is against nature: And likewise also the men, leaving the natural use of the woman, burned in their lust one toward another; men with men working that which is unseemly, and receiving in themselves that recompence of their error which was meet (Rom. 1:26-27).

For the gay person this passage, which has been traditionally interpreted as a condemnation of homosexuality, is seen as a confirmation of the homosexual's position. Gays begin with their constitutional theory—homosexuals were born this way. If they are born homosexuals, they cannot be accused of "changing their natural use which is against nature." In fact, they argue, if they try to change from being homosexual to being heterosexual, that would be against nature. Moreover, homosexuals are gentle and kind and could not be described as "consumed with passion."

In answer we might say that this argument is based on the position just mentioned, which is the most doubtful of all theories about the origin of homosexuality. There's virtually no indication to show that homosexuals were born this way, and the biological facts about men and women indicate that heterosexual relations are obviously natural relations. Paul spelled out the condemnation of homosexual relationships, which are against nature.

One fact that clearly emerges from this discussion is that a part of man's depravity is in the sexual area; and these references indicate that there were lesbian cults as well as masculine homosexual practices. All of these are viewed as leading to a final and terrible retribution.

The Pastoral Epistles

In writing to Timothy, his young son in the faith, Paul was giving him guidance about how the church is to be both organized and run. As he discussed the problems the young man would encounter, he spelled out certain kinds of people who would not recognize that their behavior was wrong. Among these were homosexuals. So Paul said that the law of God is meant to show people where they fail.

> These laws are made to identify as sinners all who are immoral and impure: homosexuals, kidnappers, liars, and all others who do things that contradict the glorious Good News of our blessed God (1 Tim. 1:10, TLB).

The homosexual advocates hasten to point out that this passage uses a word that could be translated "perverts." They claim that perversion and homosexuality are two different entities and that we should never judge homosexuality by statements about perversion. Of course, this involves a value judgment that homosexuality is OK. Any thinking, honest person, however, must surely see homosexuality as a diversion from the original biological purpose of human sexuality.

In any case, we might note that a leading minister of gay churches has a somewhat jaundiced view of Pauline theology. He declared on one occasion, "Paul did not like homosexuals" and consoled himself by saying, "We are not saved by the blood of Paul." We might answer that without Pauline theology, we would be hard put to understand all the ramifications of the blood of our Savior.

Overlooking all this rationalization, the reader notices that the purpose of this Pauline statement is to make people who have violated God's laws aware of their sinfulness. Among those who must realize that their behavior is sinful are homosexuals.

The Corinthian Passage

We have already noted the condition of Rome, but the Grecian culture in Paul's day was equally, if not more, depraved. On a hill near the city of Corinth stood the temple of Aphrodite with its thousands of corrupt priestesses. The city of Corinth became so notorious for its licentiousness that the word *Corinthianize* came to mean to act the prostitute or to be licentious. In the middle of this, Christians were warned to resist the sexual temptation of their city.

Don't you know that those doing such things have no share in the Kingdom of God? Don't fool yourselves.

> Those who live immoral lives, who are idol worshipers,
> adulterers or homosexuals—will have no share in his king-
> dom. Neither will thieves or greedy people, drunkards,
> slanderers, or robbers (1 Cor. 6:9-10, TLB).

There can be no doubt about the spiritual condition of
the homosexual. In this passage he is put in the same category as thieves, drunkards, slanderers, and robbers.

Were They Homosexual?

Not only do gay Bible students refuse to accept the obvious meaning of passages that condemn homosexuality,
but they add the unique dimension of reading into other
Bible passages a meaning never anticipated by most Bible
students. Seven relationships in the Bible are seen as homosexual.

The case of Ruth and Naomi is cited by gays as an example of lesbianism. (They note particularly the language
used in the book of Ruth ("Ruth clung to her," "she kissed
her," "she lived with her") and interpret these passages as
indicating a lesbian relation. But if there's any message in
the book about sexual relationships, it is that Naomi had
a full heterosexual relationship with her husband, giving
birth to two sons. Ruth had two husbands in succession
and gave every evidence of being a normal woman. Enroth
and Jamison have suggested that if we persist in reading
types of sexual relations into every relationship, it would
be necessary to describe Naomi as being a heterosexual who
became homosexual and then bisexual. [2] This evaluation
shows just how ludicrous these types of interpretations can
become.

Paul and Timothy are seen by the gay theologians as another example of a homosexual relationship. They notice the background alleged to give rise to homosexuality. Timothy had a strong mother and grandmother, with a weak father. Paul, the middle-aged man, is viewed as relating to the youthful Timothy in a gay manner, referring to him as "my beloved." In a letter he told him, "As I remember your tears, I long night and day to see you, that I may be filled with joy" (2 Tim. 1:4, RSV). Similarly, gays notice what they consider some gay characteristics about Paul, his advocating the kiss of greeting (Rom. 16:6) and the hugs and kisses of the church elders at the church at Ephesus (Acts 20:37). Strange—in view of the fact that they say that Paul did not like homosexuals.

The type of homosexuality the gays allegedly find in the Bible also has incestuous overtones. They conveniently find this in the case of Cain and Abel. They are particularly attracted by the statement "And unto thee shall be his desire, and thou shalt rule over him" (Gen. 4:7). This remarkable interpretation comes from a misunderstanding of a statement that the King James Version of the Bible doesn't make quite clear. The Revised Standard Version clears up the meaning: "And if you do not well, sin is couching at the door, its desire is for you, but you must master it" (Gen. 4:7). It was not Abel who desired Cain but *sin.*

Another New Testament case is an indication of the lengths gay people will go in order to bolster their case. They speak of the "gay" centurion mentioned in Matthew 8:5-13. This man's servant was healed, and the argument is that the word used for servant, *pais,* could be translated "youth" or "servant," depending on the context. Homosexuals assume that this was a case of a Roman officer and

his lover. However, the same incident is recorded in Luke's
Gospel, where the Greek word is *doulos*—a servant or slave.

Two of the relationships that gays see as homosexual
have to do with Jesus. They do not claim that Jesus was
a homosexual, but they make some interesting inferences.
Perry makes a fascinating statement:

> I do not believe that Jesus was a homosexual. But I know you people.
> Here was a guy that was raised by a mother with no father—typical of
> the homosexual syndrome, according to so many psychiatrists (for
> what that's worth)—he never married, and ran around with twelve
> guys all the time. Not only that. He wasn't above bodily contact with
> another man: John the Beloved lay on the breast of Jesus at the Last
> Supper. Not only that, but a guy betrayed him with a kiss! Doesn't
> that make you want to throw up? [3]

The apostle John is the primary suspect in having a gay relationship with Jesus. Another candidate is Lazarus—and
evidence is drawn from a noncanonical writing.

It is true that John was the disciple whom Jesus loved.
Interestingly enough, the Gospel authored by John is the
Gospel of love; but it is an *agape* love.

The gay Bible interpreters really have a field day when they
come to the relationship between Jonathan and David. Their
evidence for a gay relationship includes such things as David
loving Jonathan "as his own soul" (1 Sam. 18:1, KJV and
RSV); Jonathan's covenant with David (1 Sam. 18:3);
Jonathan stripping himself of his clothes (1 Sam. 18:4);
Jonathan delighting in David (1 Sam. 19:2); David saying,
"Your love to me was wonderful, passing the love of women"
(2 Sam. 1:26, RSV).

Amid these claims and innuendoes there are all sorts of
misinterpretations. For example, the statement that Jonathan

stripped himself of his clothes is used by some gay advocates as a basis for gay ministers practicing nudity. This is a complete misinterpretation. The Bible says nothing about being naked—simply that Jonathan passed David his robe, sword, and belt, a gift of valuable clothes. It would be natural in his position for him to give them to a close friend.

One of the claims of the gays is that David showed gay tendencies in that he could not relate satisfactorily to women. Anyone who studies David's life with an open mind could easily draw a far different conclusion. David's problem area in life was not so much that he could not relate to women but that he related a bit too well; and the great tragedy of his life came through a relationship very much heterosexual.

The David and Jonathan experience is an indication of the importance of *philia* or companionate love. In the Song of Solomon heterosexual love is presented with approval, and this passage concerning David and Jonathan is a beautiful example of the much overlooked experience of friendship. The inferences of people who must read sexual meaning into every contact between humans have helped to downgrade friendship as an experience. Let us have more genuine, vital friendships.

Examining the biblical evidence produced by the gays calls to mind the famous statement by Dr. Johnson in another context: "It's like a dog walking on its hind legs. It's not done well and one wonders why it is done at all."

Does the Bible Have a Message of Hope for the Homosexual?

Having said all this, we might now note the message of hope from the Bible. Jeff J. was a homosexual and also a professing Christian.

However, in my biblical search for a ray of hope, I did ultimately locate a helpful passage. To the church at Corinth, located in the midst of almost unimaginable sexual practices carried on by the Greeks, Paul wrote a letter saying, 'Surely you know that the wicked will not receive God's Kingdom. Do not fool yourselves: people who are immoral, or worship idols, or are adulterers, or homosexual perverts . . . none of these will receive God's Kingdom' (1 Cor. 6:9-10, TEV).

I had long realized that this was the message of the Bible, but I had missed the conclusion of the statement in the eleventh verse, 'Some of you were like that. But you have been cleansed from sin.' I never really read this statement until I saw a new translation called Good News for Modern Man. *Some friends of mine sent me a copy, and I set myself the goal of reading it through. As I read I underlined passages that were especially important to me.*

When I came to this significant statement I underlined, 'Some of you were like that.' I read and reread it. Then I broke down and cried and said, 'Thank God' because this really gave me hope. I found myself addressing the prophets of gloom: "Mr. Psychiatrist, you're wrong; Marian, you're wrong; preachers and lawyers, you're wrong." These few words from the Bible brought me new confidence. I could overcome this blight on my life.

The popular idea that the Christian religion is to condemn the homosexual and leave him without hope is not borne out in Jeff's experience. In reality, the uncompromising condemnation of the Bible helped Jeff "hit bottom" and then pushed him toward a new way of life. The same book that taught him the wrongness of homosexuality brought him his hope. His greatest encouragement and his basis for confidence in the future came from reading the Bible. Paul's letter to the Corinthians convinced him that he could be confident of beginning a new way of life. After so many disappointing experiences, the biblical statement that the Corinthians living as homosexuals had changed and were now dedicated Christians became a ray penetrating the gathering gloom.

The Bible undoubtedly has a message for the homosexual— not a message of comfort for his condition, but an unsettling message. His behavior is sinful, but he can realize, as did Jeff J., that homosexuality is a "blight on my life." He can be changed; and God, by his Holy Spirit, will help him manage his wayward sexual desires.

7. Is Gay Good?

Homosexuals themselves, although they understandably have mounted a campaign to justify and advocate the homosexual way of life, when interviewed in private often present a different perspective. In one survey three hundred homosexuals were asked, "If you had a son, would you want him to be a homosexual?" Only six answered in the affirmative.

For twenty-three years the American Psychiatric Association in its diagnostic manual listed homosexuality as a mental disorder. This evaluation was accepted across the years; but in the mid-sixties, as homosexuals became more militant, they viewed the classification as objectionable and complained about it. In December, 1973, the board of directors of the American Psychiatric Association succumbed to the pressures of the gay groups and voted to remove homosexuality from the list of mental disorders. Homosexuals were in effect declared to be normal.

It should be noted that not all psychiatrists were overjoyed by this move. Psychiatrist Socarides stated his reaction: "It is flying in the face of the one fact that we know, which is that male and female are programmed to mate with the opposite sex, and this is the story of 2½ billion years of evolution and any society that hopes to survive." Socarides added that the decision of the American Psychiatric Association was "the psychiatric hoax of the century."[1]

There may be some pretty good reasons for doubting the claim that homosexuality is normal. The word *normal* raises many problems. The confirmed male homosexual will never have the normal experiences of family relationship that are so important in the development of personality. He will not fully love a person of the opposite sex, will never know the experience of biological fatherhood and the exacting but rewarding experience of rearing one's own child.

It wasn't long before I was actively seeking homosexual contacts. Most of the time I was unsuccessful in finding them. This held true up to the time I was arrested. Probably nine out of ten times I was unsuccessful in making a contact.

I used to hang around the rest rooms, either those used by the public or in theaters. And what to the straight world must seem almost unbelievable, the courthouse rest rooms are notorious spots for rendezvous. Another place, and probably the most popular one in nearly any city because of the transient people, is the bus station rest room.

In some places there is, to use homosexual jargon, a booth with a "glory hole." That's what they call it. It is cut in the wall between the booths. Some homosexuals tell me this is the thing that excites them most. They don't even know who is on the other side.

I could never be satisfied with that. This "glory hole" may typify homosexuality. As far as my experiences are concerned, they have always been impersonal, and homosexuals who have had a wide experience say it is becoming more impersonal all the time.

Some studies have shown that many homosexuals have great difficulty in relating to anybody. Relationship is not their strong point. Sex focuses on the orgasmic moment; and many homosexuals, particularly males, are characteristically libertine. As one said, "It's much easier to deal with men than with women. You don't have to play games or strike any poses. You just side up and pop the question." Because of this casual attitude, when homosexuals do set up anything like a permanent relationship, it is frequently characterized by distrust and jealousy.

Some people may be in the wrong movement for the wrong reasons. In a day when people are seeking causes, many are tempted to align themselves with the gay movement out of sympathy for the underdog. In much the same way as a previous generation marched with black people, some people today line up with the gays.

Kids in high school today are declaring themselves to be gay. In my own counseling I have talked with kids in early adolescence who claimed to be gay; but, upon a closer examination, they turned out to be involved in fumbling efforts to discover their own sexuality. However, the idea of belonging to the gay movement apparently appealed to them, and they became a part of the activity because they were swept along with the heady feeling of helping a cause. One self-proclaimed gay frankly admitted that he never enjoyed the sexual experiences of homosexuality but went along because of the excitement of it all.

Jeff J. tells about another hazard in the homosexual way of life. The factor of homosexual violence is relatively unknown to the general public.

There were also boys whom we referred to as "rough trade"—sadists who get their kicks from beating up a homosexual. These sadistic activities are one of the most reprehensible features of the homosexual scene. An acquaintance of mine, Herman, drove up to a traffic light, and another car with a male driver drove up alongside him. Herman smiled at the driver; the man responded; and after a few signals Herman drove off, leading his pickup to the local botanical gardens, where he found a dark spot. Herman joined the other man in his car. They engaged in sexual activity.

No sooner had they concluded than Herman's erstwhile friend turned on him and bashed him up. The brawny man beat him black and blue, finally driving off and leaving him unconscious. When Herman staggered to his house that night he had two black eyes and a broken nose and was minus his wallet.

Many of the more serious people in the gay movement realize they have some strange characters in their midst. The so-called leather bars are the hangouts of sado-masochists who are capable of a wide variety of sado-masochistic practices, and the unwary person who falls into their hands will soon discover that gay is not always good.

Another less attractive side of homosexuality is the hazard of venereal disease. An investigator with the San Francisco Bay City Clinic says it is not unusual for some homosexuals to have as many as fifty or sixty contacts a month, and all of this activity has taken its toll. Amid a rising tide of venereal disease which is reaching epidemic proportions, investigators in the San Franciso area have reported that up to 40 percent of new cases of syphilis occur among male homosexuals.

Dr. Paul Popenoe, a veteran of many years of working with problems of home and family life, makes one trenchant remark about homosexuality. "Biologically, it would, of course, lead if widely practiced to the extermination of the group; and it does seem to have been at least a factor in the downfall of many cultures that tolerated it." [2] In a day when we are concerned about the quality of life, we might need to pay attention to this authority.

Another question we might ask as we evaluate homosexuality is, "What does it do to the family?" In a homosexual magazine there was actually a serious attempt to present a scheme for the artificial impregnation of lesbians with semen of high IQ males. In this way their children could be reared in the "correct" environment and conditioned to become adequate homosexuals (thus having all the enjoyments of homosexuality) and at the same time to propagate the race.

Of course we are always confronted by someone who will remind us about the "beautiful relations" possible between two people of the same sex and who will recollect two wonderful women who carried on such a relationship for so many years. While it is obvious that lesbians seem to have a somewhat different relationship from that of male homosexuals, lesbianism is not without its pitfalls. Lesbians are more likely to set up relationships of living together; but with no commitment, such as in a legal marriage, the relationship easily falls into a state of uncertainty. Horrible jealousies develop, and power struggles invade the lesbian relationship.

Two women engaged in a homosexual affair had a rupture in their relationship. Then began a strange series of events in which they did everything imaginable to embarrass each other. One of them wrote a letter of "confession," at the bottom of which she signed her former lover's name, and sent it to each faculty member of the institution from which they had graduated. The letter commenced "I am a homosexual," as she confessed for her former partner.

A teenage girl went off to an out-of-state women's university. Here she became involved in a lesbian relationship with one of her professors. The two had a disagreement; and, as a result, the girl returned home. A few weeks after her return the parents received a letter from the professor telling them all the lurid details about their daughter's lesbian escapades while she was in the university community.

One authority in the field concisely sums up the situation. "Gaining control of the partner, or gaining the assurance of being benevolently controlled by the partner, is an almost ever-present feature of the lesbian relationship. The unusual amount of hostility and even physical violence found in so many of these liaisons may be related to this struggle. One needs to control and possess, or to be controlled and possessed, and that gnawing need is often frustrated—by infidelity, rejection, or simple refusal. The result is often a seemingly irrational, uncontrollable, and infantile rage." [3]

So much for the beauties of lesbianism.

Despite my aggressiveness with men or perhaps because of it I was quite bashful with girls. Marian and I never engaged in heavy petting.

We had gone together for less than a year when we were married. I never told Marian anything about my problem for two reasons. I was afraid she wouldn't marry me if I told her. Moreover, I did not understand myself or my feelings, and I hadn't studied much about the problem at the time. Foolishly, I felt that the desire would go away once I had a normal marital sexual relationship.

Although I am a homosexual, some people might think that I am also bisexual; but in the gay world this is not considered possible. The majority of male homosexuals can perform heterosexually; however, sexual relations with men are the preferred activity. I once knew a man who, shortly after his marriage, had relations as many as four times during the day with his wife and that night would be out looking for a man.

It wasn't long before I discovered that my desire for men wouldn't go away and that my relationship with Marian didn't satisfy all my sexual longings. But I never told her.

The first few weeks of marriage we had coitus practically every night, but we soon tapered off to a couple of times a week. And I didn't want it that often. Sometimes I would give excuses for not wanting to participate in sexual activity when I knew that Marian had needs. Sometimes she cried. It made me feel bad, but not bad enough to go ahead. She thought that she might be oversexed and I was undersexed. Naturally, I knew what was wrong with me, but I wouldn't tell her.

After we had been married about four years, I decided

*one night to tell Marian everything. I waited until we had
gone to bed; then as we lay there, I said there was something that we needed to talk about. I told her about my
early homosexual experiences and the feeling I had that
something was wrong with my teenage relationships with
younger boys.*

*Marian was completely naive and very sympathetic. I
cried all the time I was talking about it, and she put her
arms around me and hugged me in much the same way
that a mother would comfort a distraught child. Marian
promised that she would love me and help me overcome
it.*

*As far as I know, Marian never read any books about
my problem and never talked to anyone who knew anything about it. She certainly was loving and kind, but I
don't think that was what I needed. She acted as if the
problem would just go away.*

*Then as the years passed she started making little jokes
when we would see someone who had effeminate characteristics. This offended me. I am not trying to blame
her, but she didn't try to learn anything about homosexuality or try to help me overcome it in any way except by assuring me of her love. Assurances were just not
enough.*

*Committed to her in marriage, with her longing for
more sexual life, I increasingly turned aside from her to
seek out the illicit and dangerous contacts of the homosexual world.*

One of the most tragic aspects of homosexuality is the invert who marries. Sometimes he takes the step in a belief that he may be able to become heterosexual once he is committed to marriage—only to discover that even though he can function in this role, his preferred sexual partners are people of his own sex. As time goes on, the invert's spouse becomes more frustrated but may have given birth to several children in the process; and she finds herself locked into an intolerable situation.

As miserable as a homosexual life-style may be in its early phases, it inevitably gets worse with each passing year.

I have often heard people talk about the fears of growing old. Believe me, the heterosexual concerns are nothing compared to those of the inverts. The elderly homosexual is a pitiful sight, particularly the one who has no money. He begs for handouts. He will give a man oral sex and then ask for a dollar, fifty cents, or even a quarter. This is the way he makes money to buy his wine. As the years go by, loneliness becomes a greater problem.

The much-touted picture of homosexuality as being an activity carried on among "consenting adults" needs some rethinking. As in all forms of sexual relationship, there is a tendency for the homosexual to turn to younger sex objects. Just take a look at the homosexual "girlie" (?) magazines and see the wide use of pictures of immature boys that are used to titillate the reader's sensuality. Investigators in large cities have discovered homosexuals

using high-school annuals and youthful procurers to make
rendezvous with high-school students. I personally have been
witness to some of this activity.

One devastating side of the homosexual scene is the number of male prostitutes for whom apparently there is a constant demand. A recent book on the subject claims there
may be more than a hundred thousand boys between the
ages of thirteen and sixteen who have generally run away
from home and who are engaged in prostitution. Police information confirms these figures, and raids have turned up
teenage brothels in Los Angeles and New Rochelle, New York.

Any discussion of homosexuality is bound to reach a point
where it focuses on the relationship of the invert to children.
The gay propagandists generally deny that this type of relationship has any significant part to play in their activities. However, when I found myself in the situation of giving a demonstration of counseling with a homosexual before a group of
counselors, I asked, "What age partners do you like best?
Do the younger ones appeal to you?"

He answered, "Of course they do. In all sexuality, even
heterosexuality, the younger sex objects are the more attractive."

In Dallas, Texas, the police became interested in the activities of one particular man who had gathered a collection of
some seven hundred pictures of nude males and females.
Following up on complaints, the police discovered that this
individual was using his "gallery" as a means of luring juveniles into his home. At one time he had twenty-five juveniles
with whom he had committed sodomy and whom he encouraged to engage in homosexual practices with each other.

In another Dallas case, three males had developed a circle
of fifty juvenile boys, who were enticed to participate in

homosexual activities while they were photographed. These pictures were then sold to distributors, and copies of them were traced to most states in the United States and abroad to Canada and Europe.

Reports of this type of activity come from different parts of the United States. One operation, described by *Time* as "a homosexual ring that would fulfill the fantasies of Marquis de Sade," came to light in Nassau County, Long Island. Four adults were arrested in connection with "a national recruitment program of young boys for the purpose of deviant sexual conduct."

The Nassau district attorney revealed that the youngsters were "bribed with very expensive gifts, clothing, as were the families of the boys. It was inferred that the recruiters were members of the Big Brother movement, since most of the boys were fatherless."

These boys, ranging in age from as young as seven years, were brought from all over the United States, Canada, Mexico, and Puerto Rico, and were seduced and trained in homosexual techniques.

Significantly, investigation revealed that few of the boys had any tendency toward homosexual conduct before they met these men and that most of them objected and had to be bribed or threatened before they finally consented to participate.[4]

Homosexuals themselves, although they understandably have mounted a campaign to justify and advocate the homosexual way of life, when interviewed in private often present a different perspective. In one survey three hundred homosexuals were asked, "If you had a son, would you want him to be a homosexual?" Only six answered in the affirmative.

Homosexuality may be a manifestation of an underlying

maladjustment. Cappon, who has written at length on homosexuality, says, "The homosexual person at best will be un-
happier and more unfulfilled than the sexually normal person
. . . . The natural history of the homosexual person seems
to be one of frigidity, impotence, broken personal relationships, psychosomatic disorders, alcoholism, paranoid psycho-
sis (i.e., the mental illness of suspicion and persecution), and
suicide." [5]

The evidence is in, and it's not a pretty picture. Despite
all the propaganda, it will still be very hard to really affirm
that "Gay is good."

8. Can Homosexuals Change?

It became increasingly clear to me that any miracle in my own life would occur as a result of day-to-day effort . . . . I had hoped for a sudden dramatic deliverance from my problem, but I realized as never before that I would have to live a day at a time. I would never be free from temptation. I would have to face each new problem situation as it arose.

A story is told about the funeral of Stonewall Jackson. One of his black servants was closely following all of the proceedings, and a visitor asked him a question: "Do you think the General will go to heaven?"

The black servant responded without a moment's hesitation, "If he wants to."

The same situation applies with the homosexual. The first and all-important question is "Does he want to change?" Not many homosexuals want to change, and this fact precludes any possibility of doing anything with them. Counseling cannot be forced upon a reluctant counselee. He must have a good, strong motivation if anything is going to happen.

If he does want to change, where will he go? One technique, known as aversion therapy, is built on the idea that homosexuality is learned behavior. In this procedure the homosexual is shown a series of homosexually stimulating pictures. As he views these pictures, he is given an electric shock. The association in the subject's mind between the stimulating pictures and the unpleasant shock may diminish his homosexual interest. However, it should be noted that many homosexuals are not disturbed by this technique.

More orthodox treatment techniques by psychiatrists

have not been notably successful; in fact, it is frequently very difficult to find some professional in the field who is willing to help homosexuals. While he was serving his sentence on the penal farm, Jeff J. received permission to visit an adult mental health clinic, where he had two sessions with the psychiatrist. Toward the end of the second session, Jeff told the doctor of his feelings about homosexuality and his hopes.

I told him also that I never really enjoyed any homosexual relationship I had for three reasons: (1) because of the fear of being discovered; (2) because I had a tremendous guilt feeling, knowing it was wrong, expressly forbidden in God's Word; and (3) because I feared Marian's reaction as well as the reaction of my church friends.

As the session came to a close, he asked how I felt they could help me. I said, "Doctor, during my imprisonment I have become painfully aware of the suffering I have caused my wife and our children, our families, and our friends. Realizing my terrible sin, I have confessed to God, and he has assured me of his soul-cleansing forgiveness. All of these things, including the prayer, thought, and Bible study I've engaged in since coming to prison, have brought me to the point where I am sure that if I went free now, nothing would ever happen again. I would not allow myself to get in a situation where I could be so tempted.

"However, I know that I am not cured yet. The emotional causes for my condition still exist. Psychiatric treatment seems to be the method that God has chosen to help me discover these causes and be rid of them so that I can think and and feel and act as a normal man again."

Returning for his third session, he had high hopes as to what was going to happen.

I was unprepared for the blow Dr. Martin delivered that afternoon. "I presented your case to the board, and we have all reached the decision that we will be unable to handle it. We feel that you should immediately begin a two-to-five year program of therapy, and we are just not equipped to handle that."

So ended my first serious attempt to obtain psychiatric help. I had started with such high hopes, and I finished with a sense of utter frustration. They seemed to be saying to me, "Well, Jeff, if you have $100,000 to spare and you can go for treatments from two to five days a week for two to five years to a psychoanalyst, it might be possible to do something for you. Might, mind you! We're not too sure."

After his release from prison, Jeff moved to a large city in another state and immediately went to the mental health center, where he had another opportunity with a psychiatrist.

When I arrived for the next session, I was encouraged to see that the psychiatrist, Dr. Harrison, was a man in his early fifties. He had twenty-three or twenty-four years in psychiatric experience and was not a forbidding person. He was, in actual fact, warm and friendly. I had the feeling that here was a man who had his own problems. He did not try to set himself up on a pedestal, pretending to be perfect. He was the type of person with whom I could share all of my feelings.

I liked Dr. Harrison and enjoyed my sessions with him. He frequently gave me valuable insights; however, if these sessions had been my only hope, I would have despaired.

I frequently had the feeling of the alcoholic and the drug addict: people who haven't been there can't have any sympathy or understanding of the problem. A straight person cannot comprehend homosexual inclinations.

On the other hand, there are homosexuals who choose to be that way; they don't want to change. They are pleased with their sexual experiences. I never was. I was unhappy in this situation.

Thinking back over my own experience, I know there must be a change of attitude toward homosexuality. An enlightened approach to the invert would involve recognition of the fact that inversion may be a symptom of an underlying emotional difficulty. Society must understand the utter futility of putting homosexuals in prison. Homosexuals should be offered treatment rather than punishment. But the big question remains: Where do we get the treatment—where?

Jeff's search then took him, of all places, to church. A visit with his pastor led to a referral to a different type of counseling center. This center was the one I direct. The support Jeff received from his counselors and from his fellow participants was the beginning of a dramatic change in him.

My new pastor was overseeing a large church and had many responsibilities, but he was very kind and took time to listen to my story. When I concluded, he told me about a counseling center in the city. Dr. Drakeford was the director, and he and the other counselors were using a new type of treatment known as Integrity Therapy. I recalled having met Dr. Drakeford when he visited at a church where I was serving, so I felt confident about meeting him.

When I arrived at the counseling center I asked to see Dr. Drakeford, but the receptionist told me he had a number of counselors working with him and I would be assigned to one of these.

It turned out to be the strangest interview I had ever experienced. The counselor, a young man, made me feel very much at ease. He sat down, asked some routine questions, and encouraged me to tell my story. To my amazement he began telling me where he had failed in his life and then went on to explain the principles of Integrity Therapy. He said that the foremost of these was responsibility. Every person who came for therapy had to accept responsibility for himself.

I had an uncanny sense of meeting someone as an equal. This man had troubles of his own and was telling me about them. I opened up and began to talk. I talked for a whole hour, keeping nothing back.

Toward the conclusion of the interview the counselor explained how Integrity Therapy operated. If I joined one of their groups, I must accept complete responsibility for my

*actions without blaming anyone else, become open before
"significant others," work on some plan of action commen-
surate with my failure, and become involved in helping
someone else with a similar problem. This was certainly
a different approach, but it made sense. I agreed to come
for at least six weeks.*

*Returning at seven o'clock that night, I encountered a
large group of people. After a short introductory lecturette by Dr. Drakeford on some aspect of Integrity Therapy,
we divided into smaller groups. I found myself sitting in a
room with four other men.*

*If somebody had said boo to me, I would have fainted
dead away. I was really scared, but I was also really de-
termined to do something about this difficulty of mine.
I had come, and I was going to follow through.*

*Fortunately, the group didn't ask me to speak that first
night. They just let me sit and listen to the others. I could
see the way the men talked about themselves and shared
their experiences. But I think that had anyone asked me
to talk about myself, I would have said, "Thank you, but
not tonight."*

*All the following week I pondered the situation. Most
of the men in the group had problems similar to mine. It
must have been as difficult for them as it was for me. Surely
I could risk being open with them.*

*The following Tuesday found me apprehensive, but ready
and willing. The leader looked at me and said, "Well, Jeff,*

why don't you tell us why you came?"

Bracing myself, I launched into my story. It took a long time—an hour or more. I was quite tearful because this was the first time I had confessed before a group of people. I went into a lot of detail, but those men listened with an intensity I had seldom seen before.

To get it all out in the open was so good. One psychiatrist has said that by confession we "throw ourselves into the arms of humanity." I certainly did that night.

Of course there was a sense in which I had previously made a confession. A man who is arrested several times and has served a prison term must have made some sort of admissions, at least to himself.

Being arrested and jailed was in itself a release to me. Perhaps there is something to the idea that the homosexual is a psychic masochist—he feels a desire to suffer for what he has done. Although I hated it for my family, my friends, and my church, my arrest brought me a strange sense of release. I was receiving the punishment I deserved; and since people knew, I no longer needed to pretend. I felt a freedom I had never known before.

However, it was not until I bared my soul to a group of people that real release came. In Integrity Therapy the group is called a "microcosm" or a "small world." The people there represented society, and I was saying, "OK, society, here I am. I've quit hiding and being secretive; this is who I am."

Group members worked at creating a free and open atmosphere. The leaders spoke about the covenant of confidentiality. No one ever repeated anything that was mentioned during a session outside the group. People were asked only their first names, and we addressed each other as Bill or Tom, etc. But I soon came to feel that this wasn't really necessary. As confidence grew, we felt perfectly free to know everything about each other. This made for a very healthy situation.

The continuing emphasis on responsibility fascinated me. In a sense I had accepted that before I ever came to Integrity Therapy. I didn't understand why I was in this condition, but I always accepted the responsibility for it. As I began to function in the group, I realized more and more the futility of blaming someone else.

I can see now that in certain subtle ways I blamed my wife for my dilemma. I often sought homosexual relationships after I had gone to a ball game or a concert or a movie. While out alone I made my most disastrous mistakes. In my strange pattern of thinking I blamed Marian because she didn't want to go anyplace with me.

I also learned in the group to face the role that deception had played in my marriage. Over and over again, I had gone out at night without telling Marian where I was going. I continually told her lies which she consistently seemed to believe. It was a painful process, but gradually I learned to accept complete responsibility for my actions.

Member of Integrity Therapy are great "actionists." Openness itself is never enough. Many a newcomer discovers to his surprise that the moment he confesses his failure, he is asked, "What are you going to do about it?" At first I was amused to hear the group making assignments for the members and then checking up the following week to see if the assignments had been completed.

"Acting as if" was a vital part of the action program. The groups had adapted a saying of E. Stanley Jones, "It's much easier to act yourself into a new way of feeling than feel yourself into a new way of acting."

A man in our group lamented that he felt his marriage had nothing in it because he did not love his wife. One particularly perceptive member asked him, "What is love?"

The leader pointed out that the word "love" is really an umbrella term including emotional reactions, companionship, and the willingness to give. He said, "Love is something you do!"

The group urged the man, "Act as if you loved your wife, and you might get to like it."

Act, act, act was the continuing refrain of Integrity Therapy.

As the weeks went by I felt more at home with the group. Three more homosexuals joined. All the leaders had experienced difficulties in the sexual area, and two of them had homosexual problems. There were people here who truly understood my problems. A feeling of confidence grew within me, and I began to say to myself, "This is the place where I am going to get some help."

*I hadn't been attending Integrity Therapy very long before
I heard the name of Dr. Hobart Mowrer. Dr. Mowrer is a research psychologist at the University of Illinois and has had
a distinguished career. In more recent days he has been moving into the area of applying his theorizing about modern
life. He has developed a unique style in group therapy, using small groups in the tradition of "self-help" groups.*

*Dr. Mowrer's work has been given a specifically religious
orientation by Dr. John W. Drakeford in his books* Integrity
Therapy *and* Farewell to the Lonely Crowd. *I soon found myself immersed in a study of these. The more I read about Integrity therapy, the better I liked it, particularly as I saw it
in practical application.*

*It became increasingly clear to me that any miracle in my
own life would occur as a result of day-to-day effort. One
evening in the lecturette preceding the session, Dr. Drakeford
spoke about the problem-solving cycle. At the time I had
hopes of reconciling with Marian, so I copied down the dia-
gram shown. (See next page.)*

*I had hoped for a sudden dramatic deliverance from my
problem, but I realized as never before that I would have
to live a day at a time. I would never be free from temptation. I would have to face each new problem situation as
it arose.*

*Preventive activity is strongly emphasized in Integrity
Therapy. Martin Luther was frequently quoted: "Don't
sit near the fire if your head is made of butter." I learned
to avoid certain situations where I might face a special
temptation.*

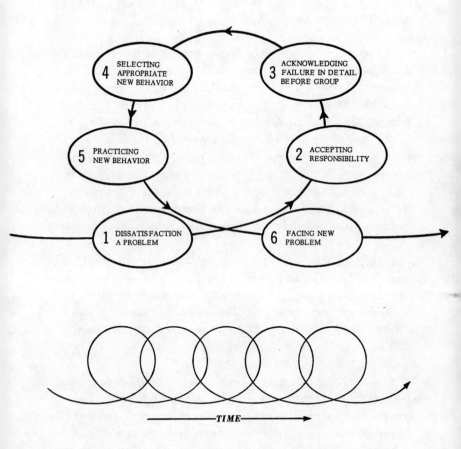

4 SELECTING APPROPRIATE NEW BEHAVIOR

3 ACKNOWLEDGING FAILURE IN DETAIL BEFORE GROUP

5 PRACTICING NEW BEHAVIOR

2 ACCEPTING RESPONSIBILITY

1 DISSATISFACTION A PROBLEM

6 FACING NEW PROBLEM

TIME

*I found meaningful support in the strength of the group.
They were with me. One of the maxims of Integrity Therapy is: "We alone can do it, but we cannot do it alone."
It was my primary responsibility, but there were other people to challenge and support me.*

*A bolder and brighter outlook came over me. Not only
was I being helped; I became aware of a growing capacity
to help others. When I first realized that I was not going
to be able to go back into church work, a sense of frustration, fear—almost terror—came over me. Then I came
to see that there was an avenue where I could help people
without being in church work. Writing a book about my
experiences, interviewing people who were counselors, and
being part of a group where I could have the opportunity
to talk with people who have the same sort of similar problems—in these ways I became involved in a helping ministry.*

*People have asked me, "How in the world do you think
you could ever be in a position to help anybody, with the
problems you have?" The person who has been there may
be of the greatest help. Dr. Drakeford has said, "No one
can speak to the homosexual the way Jeff can. I count
him my right-hand man in helping inverts."*

*In discussing Integrity Therapy many people are dis-
tressed by the emphasis on acknowledging failure. The
question is frequently asked, "Where did you go wrong?"
Some critics think these procedures will undermine the
subject's self-confidence and cause him to be overwhelmed
by a sense of inferiority. This has not been my experience.
I found that when I acknowledged my failure I lost the*

nagging sense of hypocrisy. I found myself with people who had problems of their own. No one looked down on me from his position of superiority. Then I discovered new powers—I could help somebody else. I was accepted as a leader. I had a self-esteem I had never known before. I walked with a new sense of confidence.

Jeff J. has told his own story and the difficulties he encountered when he set out to find help. If he were looking today, he would have an even more difficult time finding help. The gay movement has become so powerful that it has almost intimidated the psychological world about doing anything to change homosexuals. When psychologists have indicated they only work with homosexuals who want to change, the gays have countered that because of society's prejudice, free choice is impossible. One prominent exponent of a behavior modification technique has announced his abandonment of any techniques that "aimed at altering the choice of adult partners." [1] So it has become almost immoral to help people change.

Of course, this is nonsense. Duly considering how many people become homosexuals and the subtle pressures that were used to keep them in the gay world, they have a perfect right to decide to return to the sexual functioning God has created for them. With this in mind, the program for helping homosexuals change follows.

Help for the Homosexual

There is no sense in oversimplifying the situation; moving

from overt homosexual behavior may be a long and difficult task. For any individual, the change involves a series of steps.

1. He must have an awareness of his condition.—If this person has come out, his doing so is an acknowledgment; and he is no longer covering up his condition. He is aware of his problems, and he can do something about them.

2. He must accept responsibility.—The gay person who wants to change must be willing to forego the arguments that he was born this way, that his body chemistry caused the problem, or that his relationships with his parents were responsible. He learned this type of behavior, and he must be willing to accept his homosexuality on this basis.

3. He must have a desire to change.—This is fundamental. The conviction may come because of his religious convictions, through an awareness of the unsatisfactory nature of the gay life, or by some other means. The going will be tough, but his strong convictions may be needed to keep him moving along.

4. He should seek new company.—Peer group pressure is an important factor. Breaking with the old friends and establishing a new circle of relationships will be of great help to him. The church can and should be of primary importance to him at this stage.

5. Some type of therapy is necessary.—Therapy could be on a one-to-one basis with some professional person—however, psychiatrists don't generally have a very high batting average where homosexuality is concerned. Some type of group involvement is best, preferably with specialized groups and ex-homosexuals who are now straight.

This group will perform two functions: (1) They will be critical. They will help cut away the rationalizations the gay person builds about his behavior. (2) They will be *supportive.* As he treads his new straight path, the homosexual will pass through many periods of frustration and doubt. He needs some support. A friend whom he may call upon in his moments of difficulty will be of great value.

The group will provide a small world within which he can fully express his fears, tell of his plans, and take decisive actions, all of which are an important part of the process.

6. *He must get involved in helping someone else.*—As soon as possible he needs to get on the job of helping others. Alcoholics Anonymous has a saying, "You cannot keep your experience unless you give it away." This is equally true of the homosexual.

7. *He must face the fact.*—There is no *cure* in the sense that one will be immediately and forever delivered from his homosexuality. He will probably have some moments of temptation, but he will learn some techniques of handling his wayward sexual impulse and getting it under control.

9. The Great Propaganda Sell

*One lady was telling another, "Just imagine that,
a real live homosexual. Wasn't he brave, the way
he openly discussed his sexual activity?"*

*In the course of the interview the man admitted
deserting his wife and family, seducing boys, and
being engaged in the most far-out types of sexual
experiences. Apparently these events mattered
not at all . . . .*

When Sarah Jane Moore raised her chrome-plated .38 Smith and Wesson revolver in her right hand and supported it with her left, she took aim at President Gerald Ford. She pulled the trigger and missed, largely because a bystander named Oliver Sipple, an ex-Marine, instinctively reacted, grabbing her arm and probably saving the life of the President of the United States.

It so happens that Sipple is known in San Francisco's considerable gay community, and it is reported that two outstanding leaders of the homophile movement urged Sipple to make the most of his action to build up the image of the gay movement. To his credit, Sipple declined such a role and initiated a suit against the newspapers naming him as a homosexual, charging invasion of privacy.

The action of the gay leaders in seeking to make the most of the event by furthering their cause is typical. In part because many homosexuals seem to move into the entertainment world, they frequently have access to the media. The media have unique opportunities to get across ideas, and some homosexuals have not been slow to take advantage of the situation. In their strategic positions homosexual writers, actors, producers, and playwrights are zealously and with a sense of mission pushing their homophile philosophy.

A national television program had a homosexual theme, and at the conclusion many of the viewers paid a tribute to the skill of the propagandists when they remarked that the program was "beautifully done." Therein lies the danger. With such acceptance, more and more novels, movies, plays, and TV shows are carrying the homosexual theme.

At the not-so-subtle level of the drive come the cheap pornographic books. These are frequently stories of heterosexuals but depict the "heteros" as gradually discovering the "delights" of the distinctive homosexual activities of fellatio, cunnilingus, and anal intercourse. Then the characters find the kicks and convenience of a relationship with someone of their own sex who can provide all these types of sexual experiences without the demands that heterosexuals place on each other.

The artistic abilities so frequently found among homosexuals have not gone to waste. Great floods of visual material, explicit in its depictions of homosexual scenes and activity, have been dumped on the market. Producers of these volumes often come up with some technically good photography; but their talents are not literary, for the prose is some of the sorriest stuff that could be imagined. By and large, it seems that the main purpose for such writing is to provide a legal loophole for the publisher. If involved in courtroom proceedings, the publisher can then point to these statements as evidence that the publication has some "redeeming social value."

The United States is being flooded with pornography at this moment with the pornographic triangle—New York, San Francisco, and Los Angeles—serving as the main source, supplemented by other cities across the nation. These pornographic productions threaten to overwhelm our society. There are manifold reasons for pornography, the main one of which is the desire to turn an easy dollar. At least one other possible explanation comes from the propaganda skills of the gay world. Ordinary straight-line sexual activity is seldom the theme of pornography; it is generally perverted sexual activity. In the course of cooperating with a Christian artist, Jack Hamm, I examined thousands of pieces of pornographic literature. As I did, a new thought gradually dawned on me. The type of sexual activity generally portrayed in pornographic publications is the type of activity practiced by homosexuals.

While debate has raged over the effects of pornography, with many fervent advocates claiming that it has no effect on people, there seems to be some fairly clear evidence for another point of view. One of the most important areas of consideration is the effect of models on the reader.

When exhibitors tried to import the movie *Skyjack* in Australia, the custom and excise minister, Donald Chip, refused permission. He explained his action by saying, "The film deals with the hijacking of a crowded civil airliner by a mentally disturbed United States Army sergeant. The method of hijacking techniques employed in films are reproduced in real life a short time later."

By his action Chip was showing that he believed in imitative learning, one of the hottest ideas in the field of education today.

Edgar Guest once said, "I can soon learn if you'll show me how it's done." The older concept of apprentices working with experienced, competent mechanics, carpenters, or masons was built on the idea that the apprentice watched the master craftsman at work and learned by imitating him.

Some of the new breed of psychologists called the "behavior shapers" have been particularly enthusiastic about
these new-old techniques of learning—observing someone
else and following his example. These techniques include
modeling, vicarious learning, observational learning, and iden-
tification to describe the process.

Although Masters and Johnson used some technical procedures in their research with human sexual functioning,
when it comes to sex education they advocate a method
that is the essence of simplicity. Masters describes the teaching procedure that he suggests: "There is nothing that teaches
sex half so much as Pop patting Mom's fanny as he walks by
her in the kitchen. Obviously she loves it, and the kids watch
and say, 'Boy, that's for me.' " [1]

But what if, instead of seeing sex as part of a love relationship of two people committed to each other, the kids see a
whole variety of way-out sexual activity in which the sex of
the partner is irrelevant? Will the child not be impressed with
the ease of this expression? If some husband is feeling a bit
jaded and sees these models of sexual activity, will he not
get the idea and want to try it out? In some instances wives
are strong-armed into these types of activities, even though
they may find them repugnant.

This approach may give us a new perspective on pornography and the part that gay propaganda may play in it. It
is more than possible that homosexuals are trying to ini-
tiate heterosexual people into activities like fellatio, cunnilingus, and anal intercourse in the hope that these activities will
be widely practiced and accepted. Once there is a general
acceptance of this type of sexual congress, the gay people
will be able to say, "Why do you complain about us? The

sexual activity you are practicing—fellatio, cunnilingus, and anal intercourse—is just the same as we engage in. The only difference is that you are with the opposite sex."

A woman's magazine that presents the more obvious sexual side of feminine living has recently come out with an article on the general subject of "What Straight Women See in Gay Men." The article claims that the new freedom of homosexuals to express themselves has meant that gay men have become the coveted companions of countless women. Gays have lots of advantages as escorts: they are terrific gossips, "bitchy in a creative way," experts in advising about the clothes a woman should wear—some of them help her shop on the basis that they get a percentage of what she spends—unsurpassed as decorators, and such good confidants that a woman can feel safe and comfortable with a gay man. "I can discuss the same things I'd talk about with my mother." It's a shame the article finishes with a few lines tucked away at the conclusion telling how a girl left her gay partner at the club with his boyfriend and sat in her taxi recollecting that there were some advantages to straight men—even the worst of them. [2]

The tragedy of all this is the glamorization of homosexuality. I once gave a demonstration of a counseling technique before a large group of people—ministers, counselors, teachers, and others who are interested in marriage counseling. For the occasion a homosexual was invited in, and I carried on my counseling interview before this large group. Using the Integrity Therapy technique, I pushed him rather hard, insisting that he accept responsibility for his behavior and then eliciting details of his sexual activities. He was reluctant at first, then gradually warmed up; and the interview went about as well as one can go under such circumstances.

At tne conclusion of the session I could not help noticing the large group—mainly women—who surrounded my gay subject. One lady was telling another, "Just imagine that, a real live homosexual. Wasn't he brave, the way he openly discussed his sexual activity?"

In the course of the interview the man admitted deserting his wife and family, seducing boys, and being engaged in the most far-out types of sexual experiences. Apparently these events mattered not at all as he told about his homosexual exploits, but I could not help asking myself, *Was he really . . . brave?*

10. The Church and Homosexuality

The church will certainly have to rethink its attitude toward the homosexual. This does not mean that we have to accept the practice of homosexuality anymore than we have to accept any other sinful practice. We should love the homosexual even though we are against his homosexual practices.

The new militant movement among homosexuals has brought the church into a position where it must face the challenge of what to do about homosexuality. Many Christians find themselves on the horns of a dilemma. We function on the basis that "All have sinned and come short of the glory of God" and that Christ died for sinners. Whoever has faith in Christ is forgiven. So our churches are full of sinners. However, when it comes to the homosexual, we sometimes have difficulties in accepting him as a sinner whose sins are forgiven.

Jeff J., a Christian who was an active homosexual and turned from that way of life, reports his experience as he sensed the attitude of his fellow church members toward him.

A man stands up in church and tells the story of his early drinking escapades and slavery to alcoholism. Another admits having used drugs and tells of his struggle with addiction across the years. In both cases if the man then declares he is through with it all, he is hailed as a trophy of grace. In fact, there are preachers who travel the countryside relating the gory details of their past and drawing large crowds of hearers.

But let a man stand in church and tell about his struggle with homosexuality. A strange hush will descend. The people do not want him to go on. In fact, they generally don't want him to belong to their church. One preacher who later changed his mind said, "I thought homosexuals were just animals rather than human beings."

Why this distinction between homosexuality and other forms of deviance? Is not the alcoholic always an alcoholic, the drug addict always a potential addict? Yet on the basis of their declaration of a change of heart, they are accepted. Should not the same attitude prevail toward the homosexual? Notice that I am not pleading for the acceptance of homosexuality, just the homosexual who has had a change of heart and wants to live the straight life.

One way of coming at this problem is seen in the development of the church known as the Metropolitan Community Church, which now claims to have forty congregations spread across the country. As we have noted earlier, the leading light in all this is an ex-Pentecostal preacher who adheres to a theology that is as fundamental as any evangelical church on almost any subject except sexual behavior. These churches provide a home for the professing Christian who is homosexual but who will not or claims he cannot abandon his homosexual practices.

The idea of a gay church gives rise to some interesting possibilities. Should we have a church for all the sins that beset mankind—a thief's church, an embezzler's church, an adulterer's church, a blasphemer's church? The list could go on and on, but the idea is obviously ridiculous.

The church is a body of sinners, guilty of all types of sins; and as such, homosexuals should be welcomed. These sinners have two characteristics—they have trusted in Christ, who has forgiven them of their sins; and they are now trying, by the aid of God's Holy Spirit, to live a new life. They may fail and lapse back into sin, but they ask forgiveness and start again. Paul asked the question, "Shall we continue in sin, that grace may abound?" (Rom. 6:1). The idea is unthinkable.

The gay church is heresy. It is typical of the types of groups that have periodically arisen with a blind eye to the faults and failings dear to their hearts and have formed a religious organization that will best serve their purposes and excuse their behavior.

On the other hand, the church may be the victim of a condition sometimes referred to as *homophobia,* which is an intense fear of homosexuality. This attitude can have the effect that any close relationship between two people of the same sex is looked upon with suspicion. C. S. Lewis noticed this phenomenon and remarked, "It has actually become necessary in our time to rebut the theory that any firm and secure friendship is really homosexual." The whole situation has been complicated by the Freudians, who speak of "latent homosexuality" as a condition to be feared. Very frequently the individual so characterized has never had any homosexual experiences; but when he verbalizes an interest in someone of his own sex, the label of "latent homosexual" is applied. He ponders his situation. He has not been aware of any sexual feeling toward people of his own sex, but it may be that the professional is right. Since he just might be homosexual, he goes off to try it. This label is inaccurate, unfair, and unwarranted.

Evangelical Christians may be in a particularly difficult situation. Some unmarried young men, trying desperately to live by Christian sexual ethics, find themselves with fellow students or workmates who spend all their time planning, making, and boasting about sexual conquests. The Christian man finds his masculinity called into question and himself the recipient of not-so-subtle hints that if he does not engage in sexual seduction, he must be "queer."

Christians may have to learn to distinguish between friendship and homosexuality. When two people feel comfortable with each other and each enjoys the other's company with no sexual interest or activity, the relationship is obviously that of friendship and not homosexual. This long-range enjoyment two people have in each other's company contrasts sharply with the sexually oriented short-term relationship of the homosexual, with all the focus on the orgasmic moment.

Letha Scanzoni has brought us a feminine insight we might need in some of these relationships. She distinguishes between a "one-soul" and "one-flesh" relationship. David and Jonathan went in together as "one soul" and had a union of minds, hearts, and spirits, but not of bodies—indicating the type of relationship Jesus spoke of when he reminded man to "love his neighbor as himself."

Marriage, on the other hand, is a one-flesh relationship. As all studies have shown, this sexual factor alone will not give rise to the best relationship—it also needs to include the so-called one-soul relationship. The modern wife is not only a man's lover and the mother of his children; she is also his friend. Without this friendship, the marriage union will never realize its potential for developing the personalities of all the people who are involved.

All of this may emphasize the need we have to express our love—to tell people. One of the indications of the debasement of love is seen in the reluctance we have to tell people we love them. I once worked with a famous psychologist. Together we interviewed a depressed young lady in a hospital ward; and as we took our leave I rather impulsively said, "Remember, we love you." As we walked along, my famous friend asked, "Why did you tell her you loved her?" Without waiting to hear my answer, he went on: "Never mind about telling her—show her by what you do."

My friend had a point and gave me a jolt that stirred me into action. Just a few years later, after a very difficult period in his life, my wife and I talked with the same man on the telephone. As the conversation concluded he said, "We love you both"; and I could feel a warmth of response I had not known before. Humans need expressions of love.

The church will certainly have to rethink its attitude toward the homosexual. This does not mean that we have to accept the practice of homosexuality anymore than we have to accept any other sinful practices. We should love the homosexual even though we are against his homosexual practices. The homosexual has a special need for love, and this lack of love in life may have been a factor which helped push him toward his homosexual practice.

Christians have a commandment from their Lord, "A new commandment I give unto you, that you love one another; even as I have loved you" (John 13:34, RSV). In following our Lord's example, we should be willing to minister to people who have special needs.

One of the most exciting aspects of church life these days
is the recognition of the group we call "singles." This generally includes three types of people—those who have never
been married, those who have married and divorced, and
those who are widowed. In the past there has frequently
been the inference that because of the church's emphasis
on the family, singles didn't have a place in church life. Now
has come the new push to give singles recognition, to provide
special materials to help them, to involve them in social and
other activities in church life. My wife and I are personally
involved in family life conferences and have for some time
now included a special place for a conference for the singles.
In this conference we are emphasizing that the single is an
important part of the church family.

The church must realize that homosexuals, too, have been
unfairly treated in the past. Most of the laws and practices
which discriminate against homosexuals are obviously unfair. We should rethink our attitude toward social, econ-
omic, legislative, and political problems of the homosexual.
We gain nothing from taking a self-righteous stand in which
we just condemn the homosexual and consign him to obliv
ion, denying him even a way to earn his living.

The biggest single problem is fear. If homosexuals feel attracted to children and adolescents, it probably would not
be wise to have them working with either of these groups,
for they would be faced with a particular temptation. In the
same way as it would probably not be wise for the reformed
alcoholic to look after communion wine or a penitent embezzler to be the treasurer of the church, the homosexual
should not be placed in a position where he or she would be
confronted with special temptations. On the other hand,
there are many places within the life of the church where

homosexuals could fulfill important functions.

The whole dilemma about homosexuality may help to remind us that people have over the years become increasingly isolated. One of the good trends that may have emerged from some of the more unorthodox styles of worship is that people have become less frightened of touching each other. The increasing acceptance of people reaching out to each other might be one of the good results that has come from the encounter and sensitivity training movements. It did not come easily. Some churches told of difficulty in getting people to stand and hold hands; but once they did, people began to enjoy the experience.

In many of these trends we are rediscovering some of the ideas of the Bible. Jesus certainly touched those who were in need of healing and let John rest on his bosom. Paul followed his master's example; and when he left Ephesus, he embraced the disciples (Acts 20:1). As we noted in a previous chapter, the homosexuals have sexualized these passages and others in the Bible, reading sexual intent into them. Part of our adjustment to the new aggressiveness of the gays might well be to reclaim many of the legitimate physical contact experiences of which the Bible speaks.

A great host of people within the Christian community desperately need some sort of physical contact. Elderly people, lonely people, physically unattractive people— all have deep needs to break down their feeling of isolation. I once knew a spinster school principal in middle life. She stayed a few days in our home; and as she left, I rather impulsively put my arm around her and hugged her. Later I wondered if I'd been rather foolish and might even have offended her. However, in the letter that I received some five years after the event, she referred to "that wonderful hug that you gave me that day." Many people need someone to reach out and touch them.

It is characteristic of the ambivalence of conservative Christians in their attitudes toward homosexuality that a recent article, entitled "Gay Liberation Confronts the Church," should have made a plea for greater understanding of homosexuals.

As the article, which made many good points, progressed, the writer mentioned a plan to help homosexuals face their problem. The writer of this article is horrified by the following idea: "A Roman Catholic sociologist and priest recently suggested the formation of non-sectarian groups within the church in which homosexuals could discuss their problems. The suggestion is misguided. It makes the common mistake of attempting to find the solutions in man rather than in God. A group of homosexuals coming together to discuss their problems must necessarily talk about their sexuality. Such a discussion would be erotic rather than therapeutic for some of the participants. Small groups have been a very useful tool in the treatment of alcoholics and drug addicts. But the physical and mental conditions found in drug addiction and alcoholism are completely different from the sexual fantasy and relationships that are a part of the problems of the homosexual." [1]

Such a stance is difficult to understand. In many ways the problems of the alcoholic and the drug addict are very similar to those of the homosexual. The value of small groups is in the use of peer group pressure, the greatest human force known for changing personality. One group that has been particularly successful in dealing with homosexuals has this motto: "By relationships are they hurt; by relationships shall they be healed." Groups, like those mentioned in an earlier chapter of this book, may be the only effective human help available for the homosexual. Surely the church should plan to make such help available.

God certainly loves homosexuals. He loves all people, no matter what their faults or sins. He wants them to become his children. But God has no favorites. He has laid down his principles of living and demands that any behavior not in accord with his revelation should be abandoned. He does not tell the drunkard to abandon his drinking, the adulterer his ways, the blasphemer his blasphemy—then tell the homosexual it's OK for him to continue his deviant behavior.

When the apostle Paul asked God to remove his thorn in the flesh, the answer was, "My grace is sufficient for thee" (2 Cor. 12:19, KJV). We don't know what the thorn in the flesh was, but the answer is applicable to any problem that human beings face. As the homosexual voices his plea about his problem, the answer is forthcoming: "My grace is sufficient for thee."

Notes

Chapter 2

1. *The Catalyst*, March 11-25, 1973.

Chapter 3

1. Alfred C. Kinsey and others, *Sexual Behavior in the Human Female* (Philadelphia: W. B. Saunders Co., 1953), p. 470.

Chapter 4

1. Ibid., p. 447.
2. Ibid.
3. Ibid.
4. Fred Belliveau and Lin Ritcher, *Understanding Human Sexual Inadequacy* (New York: Bantam Books, 1970), p. 137.
5. Barry M. Dank, *Sexual Behavior*, March 1972, p. 5.
6. Wainwright Churchill, *Homosexual Behavior Among Males* (New York: Hawthorne Publishers, 1967), p. 105.

Chapter 5

1. S. Braudy, "Stalking the Wild Jill Johnston," *Ms.*, November 1975, p. 82.
2. "Gays on the March," *Time*, 8 September 1975, p. 35.
3. "The Bulldozer Rapist," *Harper's*, July 1975, pp. 6-7.
4. Kinsey, p. 458.
5. "When Women Love Other Women," *Redbook*, November 1971, pp. 84-85.
6 David Reuben, *Everything You Always Wanted to Know About Sex But Were Afraid to Ask* (New York: Bantam Books, 1970), p. 269.
7. Ibid., p. 272.
8. Sally Gearhart and William R. Johnson, *Loving Men/Loving Women* (San Francisco: Glide Publications, 1974), p. 136.
9. Ibid., p 134

10. Ibid., p. 128.
11. Ibid., pp. 126-127.
12. Ibid., p. 127.
13. Ibid., p. 128.

Chapter 6

1. Troy Perry and Charles L. Lucas, *The Lord Is My Shepherd and He Knows I'm Gay* (Los Angeles: Nash Publishing, Inc., 1972), p. 150.
2. Ronald M. Enroth and Gerald E. Jamison, *The Gay Church* (Grand Rapids: Eerdmans Publishing Company, 1974), p. 55.
3. Perry and Lucas, p. 152.

Chapter 7

1. "An Instant Cure," *Time,* April 1974, p. 45.
2. Paul Popenoe, "Are Homosexuals Necessary?" *Publication 452* (Los Angeles: The American Institute of Family Relations).
3. Belliveau and Ritcher, pp. 54-55.
4. "White Slavery, 1972," *Time,* 5 June 1972, p. 24.
5. Daniel Cappon, *Toward an Understanding of Homosexuality* (Englewood Cliffs, New Jersey: Prentice Hall, Inc., 1965), p. 115.

Chapter 8

1. Kenneth Goodall, "The End of Playboy Therapy," *Psychology Today*, October 1975, p. 59.

Chapter 9

1. Belliveau and Ritcher, p. 219.
2. "What Straight Women See in Gay Men," *Cosmopolitan*, October 1975, p. 540.

Chapter 10

1. Guy Charles, "Gay Liberation Confronts the Church," *Christianity Today*, 12 September 1975, p. 17.